When FOOTBALL Was FOOTBALL

LIVERPOOL

© Haynes Publishing, 2010

The right of Peter Hooton to be identified as the author of this Work has been asserted by him in accordance with the Copyright, Designs & Patents Act 1988.

First published in 2009

A catalogue record for this book is available from the British Library

ISBN: 978-1-844258-25-3

Published by Haynes Publishing, Sparkford, Yeovil,
Somerset BA22 7JJ, UK
Tel: 01963 442030 Fax: 01963 440001
Int. tel: +44 1963 442030 Int. fax: +44 1963 440001
E-mail: sales@haynes.co.uk
Website: www.haynes.co.uk

Haynes North America Inc., 861 Lawrence Drive,
Newbury Park, California 91320, USA

All images © Mirrorpix

Creative Director: Kevin Gardner
Designed for Haynes by BrainWave

Printed and bound in Britain by J F Print Ltd., Sparkford, Somerset

When FOOTBALL Was FOOTBALL

LIVERPOOL

A Nostalgic Look at a Century of the Club

Peter Hooton

Contents

Introduction

This book is a unique and magnificent collection of photographs of Liverpool Football Club from the birth of the club in 1892 until 1992 the club's centenary, selected from thousands of images in the *Daily Mirror's* extensive archive. Many of these superb images are previously unpublished and document the rise of the most successful football club in the English game. From the early days and the championship winning sides of the early 1900s to 'The Untouchables' of the 1920s, to the coming of the 'messiah' Bill Shankly in 1959 after the lean years of the 1930s, '40s and '50s, it's all here. From the triumphs of the '60s '70s and '80s to the tragedies of Heysel and Hillsborough this book will bring to life the periods, the personalities and the human stories.

Evocative images of Liverpool FC 'icons' throughout the 20th Century from the early days to the dawning of the Premiership. Legends such as international keeper Elisha 'the panther' Scott, to 1930s captain Matt Busby, yes Matt Busby! The book illustrates and documents 1950s heroes Billy Liddell and Albert Stubbins to the architects of Liverpool successes since the 1960s, Bill Shankly, Bob Paisley, Joe Fagan and Kenny Dalglish. The triumphs, the trophies and the stars such as Roger Hunt, Ian St John, Emlyn Hughes, Tommy Smith, Ian Rush, Graeme Souness, and John Barnes are all featured.

Liverpool Football Club is more than a club though, it is an institution and at its heart and soul are the fans and in particular the Spion Kop. Famed throughout the world the travelling fans are captured at home and abroad featuring changing terrace fashions to celebrations in far off lands!

When Football Was Football – Liverpool is a splendidly illustrated book with a commentary from a lifelong Liverpool fan Peter Hooton who has been an eyewitness to many of the triumphs and the tragedies since the 1970s. Supporting Liverpool is in Peter's blood as both his father and grandfather were big fans of the 'Reds'. His granddad actually took him the short distance to Anfield from his home in the area for the first time to watch the reserves, during the Shankly era, and his dad played for the Oakfield Pub a stones throw from the Anfield stadium in the 1950s and has been a season ticket holder at Anfield since the early 1960s.

After seeing and reading this book you will have a window into the fascinating story of one of the most famous football clubs in the world! This is the story of Liverpool Football Club, When Football Was Football from the heart of the city!

Above: Peter Hooton's dad highlighted playing for the Oakfield Pub team from Anfield in the 1950s.

Below: Peter Hooton's granddad highlighted when playing for Nash Grove AFC in the 1906-7 season after they had just won the Kensington Amateur League Cup.

Players, back row, left to right: John McCartney, Matthew McQueen, Andrew Hannah (captain), Billy McOwen, Duncan McLean, Douglas Dick, David Henderson. **Front row, left to right:** Patrick Gordon, Malcolm McVean, Joseph McQue, James McBride, Harry Bradshaw, Jimmy Stott, Hugh McQueen. John Houlding is seated in the centre.

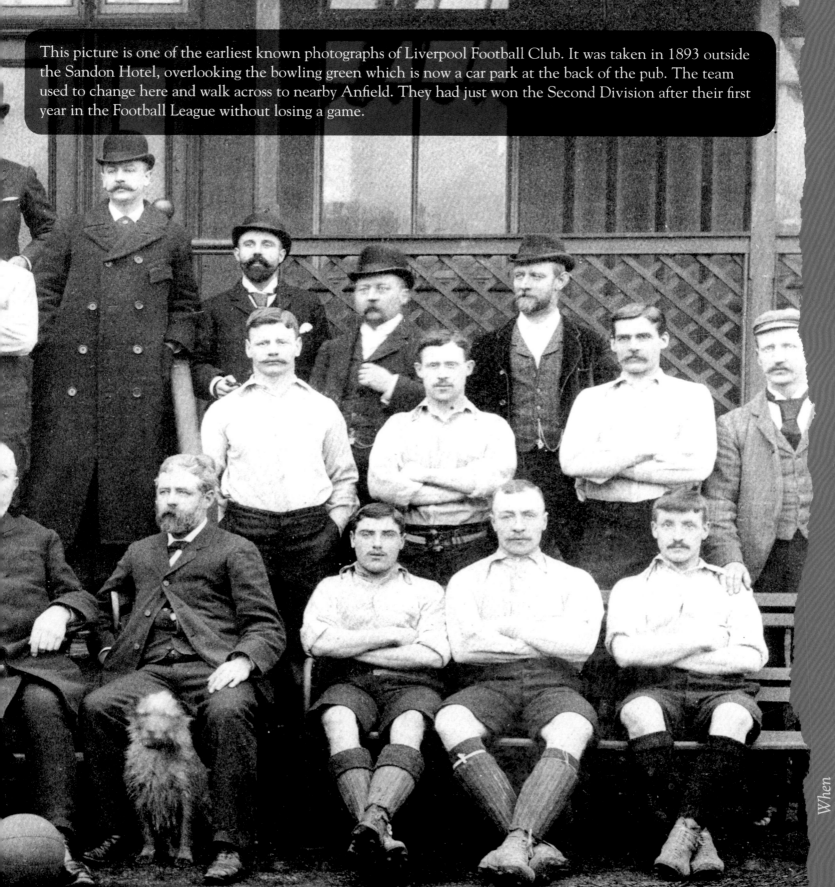

This picture is one of the earliest known photographs of Liverpool Football Club. It was taken in 1893 outside the Sandon Hotel, overlooking the bowling green which is now a car park at the back of the pub. The team used to change here and walk across to nearby Anfield. They had just won the Second Division after their first year in the Football League without losing a game.

John Houlding, brewer, entrepreneur, politician and founder of Liverpool Football Club.

The Founding of the Football Club

John Houlding was the founder of Liverpool Football Club. "King John", as he was known, had actually been the driving force behind Everton FC. Houlding had made his fortune out of the brewing business but he also had a keen interest in sport. His Anfield Road house overlooked Stanley Park, and he would watch matches from his elevated rear terrace every weekend. Teams would come from all over the city to play football as the game's popularity increased. It was a club called Everton, formerly St Domingo Football Club, that captured his imagination and he soon began to invest his money into the club, eventually renting a plot of land between Walton Breck Road and Anfield Road for the team to play. The first match took place here in September 1884 at what later became known as Anfield. When professionalism was introduced into the game in 1885 Everton's players went full time and three years later they were the founding members of the English Football League.

There were other prominent local clubs like Bootle FC and Liverpool Ramblers, but under Houlding's leadership Everton prospered and became the dominant force. When Everton won the League in 1891, simmering Board Room tensions erupted into open rebellion when Houlding increased the annual rent on the Anfield ground, which he now owned outright. But this was by no means the only reason for the fall-out. Everton still had a number of strict Methodists on their Board who, as active and vociferous members of the Temperance Movement, saw alcohol as one of the reasons for the city's problems. They particularly disliked Houlding because of his vigorous promotion of alcohol; not only was he chairman of the Liverpool Brewers Association, he also opposed a local by-law making it illegal for pubs to serve alcohol to children under 13 and led a campaign

Liverpool FC won the First Division championship in 1900-1 after less than 10 years in existence.

to allow pubs to keep their back doors open all day.

Members were also unhappy that the team still had to get changed in one of his pubs, the Sandon Hotel, and walk the short distance over to the ground; they thought this was unprofessional and was a way of Houlding attracting fans to drink in his pub. As well as attempting to raise the rent on the ground, Houlding also insisted that only his beers would be available for sale at Anfield in the coming season. So even in those days commercialism and business interests were major footballing concerns. A crisis meeting was held in March 1892, but the relationship between "King John" and most of the Everton members was beyond repair and all but a handful of loyalists decided to leave for the Mere Green field, which would later become Goodison Park. Houlding felt he had been betrayed as he had built Everton up from virtually nothing, investing large sums of his own money for modest returns.

Though many people had given up on the game, John Houlding remained undaunted and decided to build a new club – an institution that would become one of the most famous football clubs in the world.

Only a few days later, at a meeting at his Anfield Road home, Houlding attempted to carry on a newly formed club with the same name – Everton – but the Football League rejected his plan, ruling that the name Everton should stay with the existing team and the majority of members who had walked out of Anfield. The small band of Houlding loyalists, which included just three players, decided they would need a name that would inspire and attract support from all over the city; and so on 15 March 1892 Liverpool Football Club was born.

John McKenna.

After being accepted into the Football League in 1893 to play in the newly formed Division Two, Liverpool were promoted in their first season to Division One but soon fell back to the Second Division the following year. In 1897 they were back in the top flight and had recruited Tom Watson, who was regarded as one of the best coaches in the country. His first major signing was Alex Raisbeck, who joined Liverpool from Stoke City in the summer of 1898. This signing played a major part in Liverpool winning their first championship in 1900-1 and he was a dominant force in the heart of the Liverpool defence for just over a decade.

John McKenna was from County Monaghan in Ireland. He came to Liverpool as a teenager and although he started off as a grocery boy, through sheer hard work and determination he became a rich man. He became a good friend of John Houlding and was a regular at Anfield to watch Everton. When the split came, Houlding made McKenna a director of Liverpool Football Club and he soon became the driving force behind the scenes. Having made two tours to Scotland to recruit players for the new club, the team had so many Scottish players it became known as the "team of the Macs". Nicknamed "Honest John", McKenna was a tireless servant and chairman to both Liverpool Football Club and the Football League.

–LEGENDS–

Alex Raisbeck

Alex Raisbeck was bought from Stoke City for £350 in 1898. A commanding defender, he became one of Liverpool's first stars, helping them lift the First Division championship in 1900-1 and 1905-6. Although he was not tall for a defender, standing just less than 5ft 10ins, he was dominant in the air and skilful on the floor. He captained the side for many years and his energy and leadership was an inspiration to his team-mates.

FOOTBALL –STATS–

Alex Raisbeck

Name: Alexander Galloway Raisbeck

Born: Polmont, Stirlingshire 1878

Died: Liverpool 1949

Position: Centre-half

Liverpool Playing Career: 1898-1909

Club Appearances: 340

Goals: 21

Scotland Appearances: 8

Goals: 0

Action from the first day of the 1905-6 season. Even though Liverpool lost 3-1 to Arsenal in front of a crowd of 20,000 and also lost the next two games, they went on to win the League.

Liverpool Second Division champions, 1904-5.

In the end Liverpool won the League with relative ease after a terrific mid-season run of 11 games unbeaten, 9 wins and 2 draws. Their nearest challengers, Preston North End, were beaten 2-1 at Deepdale, which more or less settled the issue.

–LEGENDS–

Sam "Chuffer" Hardy

Sam Hardy played for Chesterfield against Liverpool in the 1904-5 season and conceded six goals. But he caught the eye of the Liverpool staff, that spotted his potential. He signed for Liverpool soon after for £500, and he went on to become one of the outstanding goalkeepers of that period. In all he won 14 England caps while playing for Liverpool and helped win the First Division championship in 1905-6. He was nicknamed "safe and steady Sam".

"Sam Hardy was one of the greatest goalkeepers I ever saw play," Jesse Pennington England and West Brom full-back.

OGDEN
CIGARE

FOOTBALL –STATS–

Sam Hardy

Name: Samuel Hardy

Born: Chesterfield 1883

Died: Chesterfield 1966

Position: Goalkeeper

Liverpool Playing Career: 1905-1912

Club Appearances: 239

Goals: 0

England Appearances: 21

Goals: 0

The Daily Mirror

LATEST CERTIFIED CIRCULATION MORE THAN 900,000 COPIES PER DAY.

No. 3,278. — Registered at the G.P.O. as a Newspaper. — MONDAY, APRIL 27, 1914. — One Halfpenny.

THE ROYAL CUP FINAL: THE KING PRESENTS TROPHY TO BURNLEY CAPTAIN.

The King handing the English Cup to Boyle, the Burnley captain.

Sewell, the Burnley goalkeeper, makes a wonderful clearance.

The King and the Lord Mayor of London, Sir T. V. Bowater, watching the game.

Panoramic view of the Crystal Palace ground taken while the match was in progress.—(*Daily Mirror* photograph.)

For the first time in history, a British monarch was present at the Cup final, which was played at the Crystal Palace on Saturday in the presence of an enormous concourse of spectators. Two Lancashire clubs, Burnley and Liverpool, were engaged in the struggle, which resulted in a win for the former eleven by one goal to nothing. At the end of the game Boyle, the captain of the Burnley team, was presented to the King, who handed him the English Cup.

14

"The Husband She Bought": Our Serial Which Appeals to Everyone

BEAUTIFUL Photographs of Miss Gladys Cooper in "My Lady's Dress."

The Daily Mirror

LATEST CERTIFIED CIRCULATION MORE THAN 900,000 COPIES PER DAY.

THE KING Presents the English Cup to Boyle, the Burnley Captain.

THE ENGLISH CUP FINAL AND HOW SOME OF THE SPECTATORS SAW IT.

The only goal of the match, which was scored by Freeman (x). One of his colleagues is seen running towards him to congratulate him.

Sheldon intercepts a pass to Freeman (Burnley).

An anxious moment for Liverpool's goalkeeper.

Campbell, Liverpool's custodian, saving from Freeman.

One of the Burnley backs clearing with his head.

Necessity the mother of invention.

Balancing on beer bottles.

Sailors up a tree.

Comfort sacrificed to fine view.

Comfort was not studied by the spectators at the Crystal Palace who were ready to suffer any inconvenience to get a good view. To climb a tree was an easy task for sailors, but the girl who balanced herself on the necks of two beer bottles performed quite a clever feat.—(Daily Mirror and C.N.)

Printed and Published by THE PICTORIAL NEWSPAPER CO. (1910), LTD., at THE Daily Mirror Offices, 23-29, Bouverie-street, London, E.C.—Monday, April 27, 1914.

In the 1913-14 season Liverpool had a disappointing time in the League but they did reach the Cup final in April 1914, which was held at Crystal Palace. It was the first Cup final attended by the King and was to be the last before the First World War. Liverpool lost to Burnley 1-0 in front of a crowd of over 77,000.

–LEGENDS–

Don McKinlay

One of the many Scots who played for Liverpool over the years, Don McKinlay captained the Liverpool "Untouchables" team that won two consecutive championships between 1921 and 1923. He was a powerful left-sided player but he was also a "utility" player who occupied nearly every position over the years. As a fierce tackler not much got past him, but he was also keen to get forward and score goals. He even replaced Elisha Scott in goal once after Scott was injured in a friendly match. His career spanned almost 20 years and he retired through injury to become a publican in Liverpool.

FOOTBALL –STATS–

Don McKinlay

Name: Donald McKinlay

Born: Glasgow 1891

Died: Liverpool 1959

Position: Left-back or Left-half (midfield)

Liverpool Playing Career: 1910-1929

Club Appearances: 433

Goals: 34

Scotland Appearances: 2

Goals: 0

FOOTBALL –STATS–

Harry Chambers

Name: Henry Chambers

Born: Northumberland 1896

Died: Shrewsbury 1949

Position: Inside-forward

Liverpool Playing Career: 1919-1928

Club Appearances: 338

Goals: 151

England Appearances: 8

Goals: 5

H. CHAMBERS
LIVERPOOL

–LEGENDS–

Harry Chambers

Henry "Harry" Chambers was a shipyard worker by trade and was nicknamed "Smiler". He had a tremendous goalscoring record at Anfield and scored a memorable hat-trick against Everton in a 5-1 win in October 1922. With his stocky frame and distinctive bow legs he scored on average a goal every two games and was instrumental in helping the Liverpool team win the First Division championship in two consecutive seasons in the early 1920s. He had a terrific shot and was Liverpool's leading goalscorer in the first five seasons after the First World War. He was transferred to West Bromwich Albion in 1928 for £2,375 where he played at centre-half for the remainder of his career.

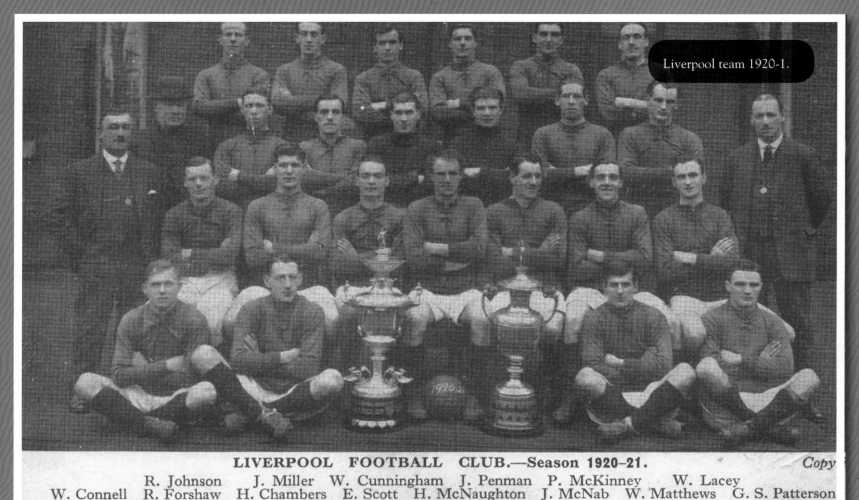

LIVERPOOL FOOTBALL CLUB.—Season 1920–21. *Copy*

R. Johnson   J. Miller   W. Cunningham   J. Penman   P. McKinney   W. Lacey

W. Connell   R. Forshaw   H. Chambers   E. Scott   H. McNaughton   J. McNab   W. Matthews   G. S. Patterson
(*Trainer*)   (*Secretary*)

D. Ashworth (*Manager*)   J. Sheldon   J. Bamber   T. Lucas   E. Longworth   D. McKinley   T. Bromilow   A. Pearso

R. Jones   W. Jenkinson   (*Lancashire Cup*)   O   (*Liverpool Cup*)   H. Lewis   H. Wadsworth

After the First World War, Division One was expanded to 22 teams and the players maximum wage was raised to £9 per week. The 1919-20 season saw attendances booming with Liverpool averaging 40,000 every week. In the third round FA Cup match against Birmingham 50,000 crammed into Anfield.

In the first two seasons after the war Liverpool finished a creditable fourth on both occasions and there was a feeling of expectancy around Anfield that the team would be challenging for honours soon. With David Ashworth becoming manager in 1920 the club had a new vision and new focus. Liverpool had been managerless since the death of previous manager Tom Watson in 1915 and team selection and recruitment had been left to the directors and training left to ex-players.

By the 1921-2 season Liverpool were indeed challenging for the League with pre-war players like Longworth, McKinlay, Lacey and Sheldon joined by new arrivals like Geordie Harry "Smiler" Chambers and Widnes-born inside-forward Dick Forshaw. Liverpool-born stylish wing-half Tom Bromilow was regarded as the brains behind the team and the Liverpool team of the early 1920s were known as "The Untouchables".

Liverpool's strength was based on a solid defence and especially the goalkeeping of Elisha Scott.

Right: Scott, of Liverpool (right), runs out to clear an Everton attack. Liverpool won by 5 goals to 1.

Grimsdell (left white shirt), the Spurs' captain, heads away from a corner-kick by Liverpool. The League leaders won 4-2.

McKinlay (centre), Liverpool's left-back clears when pressed by Aitken of Newcastle.

Action from the Liverpool v Burnley game played at Anfield in front of 45,000. Liverpool continued their good form and won the game 3-0 with two goals from Forshaw and one from Chambers.

-LEGENDS-

Elisha Scott

Elisha Scott was a Liverpool and Northern Ireland goalkeeping legend and is regarded as one of the best goalkeepers of all time. After keeping a clean sheet for Liverpool on his debut against Newcastle at St James's Park on New Year's Day 1913, he went on to make 468 appearances for "the Reds" spanning three decades, from 1912 to 1934.

Born in Belfast he played for Belfast Boys Brigade as a junior and Linfield of Belfast, who decided that at just over 5ft 9ins tall he was too small to make a goalkeeper. Scott came from a footballing family, and his elder brother, Billy, actually kept goal for Everton in the early 1900s. Everton were interested in Elisha but they felt he was too young and inexperienced for them. Thankfully, Liverpool had no such reservations and their confidence was more than justified.

The Anfield faithful adored "Lisha", who was ever present in the League championship, winning the sides of 1921-2 and 1922-3. It is said that he commanded his defence with authority and was not loath to using "industrial" language to get his point across to his team-mates.

> *He had the eye of an eagle and the swift movement of a panther... and the clutch of a vice when gripping the ball.*
> *Liverpool Daily Post & Echo*

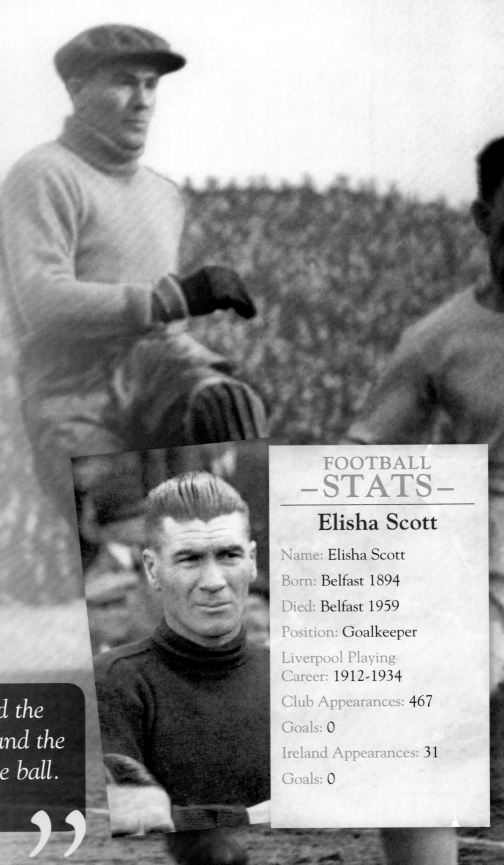

FOOTBALL -STATS-

Elisha Scott

Name: Elisha Scott

Born: Belfast 1894

Died: Belfast 1959

Position: Goalkeeper

Liverpool Playing Career: 1912-1934

Club Appearances: 467

Goals: 0

Ireland Appearances: 31

Goals: 0

Liverpool goalkeeper Elisha Scott clears the ball after a shot from Huddersfield Town player Meads during a match under wretched conditions at Leeds Road in 1927.

Chelsea's defenders on the alert while Forshaw of Liverpool heads the ball over. Liverpool won the game 1-0.

Liverpool's defence hard-pressed by Sheffield United, winners by the odd goal in three.

TO-DAY'S FOOTBALL.

Arsenal's Attractive Home Game with Aston Villa.

LIVERPOOL'S TASK.

At home to Aston Villa, Arsenal have the most attractive fixture in London this afternoon, though many will prefer the local Derby between Crystal Palace and West Ham at Selhurst. Other League games in the metropolis this afternoon are Fulham v. Leeds, Brentford v. Bristol City and Charlton v. Swansea.

Arsenal will have to put their best foot forward to repeat last season's 2—0 victory against the Villa, as the latter have a great opportunity of challenging Sunderland for the distinction of being runners-up.

The home team have one advantage—they will start fresher than their opponents. The Highbury side did not meet anyone yesterday, whereas the Villa extended themselves against Chelsea, so perhaps, with this factor in their favour, the points may remain in town.

Liverpool, champions as well as prospective champions, may have to be content with a point against Birmingham, who are in so parlous a state that they are certain to battle hard for a share of the spoils, at least. A draw is the result indicated.

FINALISTS SHOULD WIN.

Blackburn Rovers and Bolton Wanderers should each record home victories. The former meet Oldham, who seem to have only a remote hope of escaping relegation, while Middlesbrough have cracked up so badly in the last few weeks that their chances against the Cup finalists appear meagre.

After their great performance yesterday Cardiff will start hot favourites for their match with Preston North End, especially as Preston will be without McCall, who was injured at White Hart-lane.

Everton find Burnley in a somewhat subdued mood, and should win with something to spare, while Huddersfield are doing well enough to suggest the possibility of their success at home against Newcastle United.

Chelsea had a hard game with Aston Villa yesterday, and will therefore have hardly expect to succeed against Manchester City. The Pensioners are dead out of fortune this season. David Calderhead will tell you there are now three sorts of luck—bad luck, very bad luck, and Chelsea's. Perhaps he's right.

Stoke should beat Nottingham Forest, but the Spurs may hold Sunderland to a division of honours. They went North after yesterday's match with Preston, and will stay there until after Monday's game at Preston. West Bromwich Albion and Sheffield United should provide a close game, in which ground advantage should tell in favour of the Throstles.

IN THE SECOND DIVISION.

West Ham will have to fight hard for success against Crystal Palace, but the Cup finalists may bring it off. Burnley on form should account for Coventry City, but the probable outcome of the clash between Blackpool and Manchester United is a draw.

Round Homerton way they will tell you they are confident of escaping relegation, but their hopes against Derby County can be but small. Fulham have in Leeds a body of opponents with an almost identical League record, but ground advantage should turn the scale in their favour.

In the Third Division, Bristol City should beat Brentford at Griffin Park, as the home club are very much in the doldrums. Bristol Rovers and Swindon are very close rivals, and a draw should be the outcome of their meeting at Eastville. A similar result may be expected from the clashes between Charlton and Swansea and Exeter and Luton.

Queen's Park Rangers, strengthened by the return of Bain, will run Merthyr close, but the Welshmen are stronger now than they have been at any time this season, and might just scrape home. Millwall will find Northampton a difficult side to beat on their own pitch, while Plymouth will not fear for their home record of two seasons' standing as a result of the visit of Aberdare.

LIVERPOOL AGAIN.

West Ham Still in the Running for the Double Event.

For the first time in their thirty-seven years of existence the London Caledonians have won the Amateur Cup. They have always been in the forefront of amateur football, but the supreme honour has hitherto been denied them. The weather on Saturday, although cold, was excellent for outdoor sports, and golf, athletics and football were in full swing, although there was an end of the season touch about the last-named game. Chief features of Saturday's sport were:—

Football.—Liverpool made themselves champions for the second year in succession; West Ham kept themselves in the running for promotion by beating Fulham, and Bristol City won the championship of the Southern Third Division.

Racing.—Favourites fared badly at Derby, where Dawn of Peace gained a clever victory in the chief handicap at the expense of Sprig of Orange.

CALIES' TRIUMPH.

Amateur Cup Brought South by the Scots.

London Caledonians won the Amateur Cup for the first time in their history on Saturday, when they beat Evesham by two goals to one, after extra time.

There was rare enthusiasm on the ground among the 14,000 spectators. Evesham had not obviously been beaten this season.

Evesham, sturdy and solid, rather put the faster and cleverer Scots off their game by the whole-hearted vigour of their methods, and play as fierce rather than spectacular.

The Calies started well against the wind. Stokes and Bridges, the Evesham backs, were shaky in defence, and Sloan, catching them in two minds, dashed through and scored.

JONES EQUALISES.

This only served to put Evesham on their mettle. Osborne, at outside left, did some bright things, and the brothers Gates were harassed in defence. Still they held out, and Lawson, in goal, made some brilliant clearances before S. Jones headed a grand goal.

Calies seemed to falter in the second half, and but for the fact that Dawson made some fine saves from Busby and S. Jones, and the Gates were again at their best, the "village lads" might have won.

Extra time had to be played, and the Calies seemed to get their second wind. They rearranged their forward line, and, following smart play by Blyth, McCubbin was given an opening to win the match with a good goal.

It is not out of turn for the Calies, a club in their thirty-seventh year, to have won the Cup at last. The receipts were £1,177.

CHAMPIONS AGAIN.

Liverpool Join a Select Band of Successful League Clubs.

By taking a point from Huddersfield while Sunderland were losing at Burnley, Liverpool join a select band of clubs with the distinction of having won the League championship in successive years.

The feat has not been achieved since Sheffield Wednesday accomplished it in the seasons 1902-3 and 1903-4—just twenty years ago. Preston North End have done it; so have Sunderland. Aston Villa are the only club to do it twice, and that with only one season between the double event. It is the fourth time the honours of the competition have been won by the Merseyside club—they are worthy winners. Easily the most consistent side in the country, they are also the best balanced. It is impossible to pick out one or two men and say: "These are the stars of the side." It is, rather, a team of stars; a team in which every man is a master of his craft.

The Liverpool match attracted 35,000 people, who see the Anfielders gain their coveted distinction. They were kept on tenterhooks to the end, last year's Cup-holders were a goal ahead until five minutes from time, thanks to a goal from Chambers that appeared to enter the net off one of the home defenders, leaving Elisha Scott quite sighted.

Liverpool played with grim desperation in the closing stages to get on terms, and it was from one of Lacey's perfectly-timed centres that Sturgess headed through the goal that brought the point which meant so much to the champions. Liverpool well deserved the equaliser. Sunderland or Huddersfield will be runners-up.

STURGESS' VALUABLE GOAL.

The Wearsiders have the greatest chance they are performing below their best just now, and were beaten on Saturday at Burnley by two clear goals. Kelly and Freeman scoring.

Far Left: Liverpool beat Sheffield United 2-1 in the League with two goals from Chambers and strengthened their position at the top of the League with only six games to play.

Left: Liverpool playing Birmingham at home: even though they only managed a 0-0 draw they still looked likely League winners.

Below: "The Untouchables" are champions again!

THE DAILY MIRROR, Monday, April 3, 1922.

| DAILY MIRROR FASHION FAIR HOLLAND PARK HALL OPENS ON APRIL 16. | Molly's Bed of Earth: See Page 13 | MUTT AND JEFF WILL MAKE YOU LAUGH. SEE PAGE 19. |

The Daily Mirror

NET SALE MUCH THE LARGEST OF ANY DAILY PICTURE NEWSPAPER

LEAGUE FOOTBALL, RUGBY AND RACING FIGURE IN WEEK-END SPORT PROGRAMME

Johnson, of Cardiff, tackling a Newport three-quarter in their Rugby match at Cardiff. Once again neither team scored.

The field together just after the start of the Enfield Plate at Alexandra Park.

Blake, the Tottenham goalkeeper, fisting clear after a corner-kick. Sunderland scored the only goal of the game.

Miss Hill, on Pharaoh's Daughter, winning a race at the Red Roar Hunt's point-to-point steeplechases at Great Leighs.

A tete-a-tete between Johnson, of Liverpool, and McClure, of Birmingham. No score.

A misunderstanding in Manchester United's goal enables Blackpool to open the scoring. Manchester won 2—1.

Chelsea player heading against Manchester City. Result one all.

Bristol's Rugby match with Harlequins, who won by 10 pts. to 10.

The League championship is still undecided, though four weeks more will see the close of the football season. Liverpool are likely to retain the title, but there is just sufficient doubt to sustain a lively interest in the performance of the leading clubs. At the other end of the table is keen competition to escape relegation. (Daily Mirror photographs.)

Printed and Published by The Daily Mirror Newspapers, Ltd., at 33-35, Bouverie-street, London, E.C.4.—Monday, April 3, 1922. Telephone Central 9600.

—LEGENDS—

Tom Bromilow

Local lad Tom Bromilow was regarded as the brains behind "The Untouchables" side of the early 1920s. He was originally invalided out of the army with septic poisoning but recovered enough to go to Anfield and ask for a trial. Liverpool accepted and Bromilow immediately impressed, signing as a professional in April 1919. He was a fine tackler and superb passer of the ball, and within two years of his trial at Anfield he was playing for England. After his playing career was over he went into management and had spells at Burnley, Crystal Palace and Leicester City.

KEEPS YOU IN TIP-TOP FORM

England's International Player

T. G. Bromilow, Liverpool Football Club, writes :—"To-day football calls for a greater amount of physical exertion than ever, on account of the marked increase in the speed of the game and the extension of the league programme. The player who lacks pace and stamina is very noticeable, and quickly singled out. It is absolutely essential that a player must be in the best possible condition to keep time with the present football speed. Personally, I have found that Phosferine is responsible for my attaining this end, it being

A GREAT STIMULANT TO THE NERVES,

is highly revitalising, and after a particularly strenuous game, Phosferine positively prevents any of that feeling of nerve exhaustion which is usually the forerunner of a legion of nerve disorders, Influenza, etc.

The more things change the more they stay the same. The only difference being the sums of money involved!

Even in those days famous players were endorsing products. The Liverpool and England left-half Tom Bromilow advertised "Phosferine", a cure-all tonic.

GENERAL EXHAUSTION
AND RE-VITALISES THE WHOLE NERVE SYSTEM

FOOTBALL —STATS—

Tom Bromilow

Name: Thomas George Bromilow

Born: Liverpool 1894

Died: Nuneaton 1959

Position: Left-half

Liverpool Playing Career: 1919-1930

Club Appearances: 375

Goals: 11

England Appearances: 5

Goals: 0

The 1930s

Liverpool football team of the 1930-1 season pose for a group photograph in August 1930. **Back row, left to right:** Hodgson, Gardner, Bradshaw, Scott, the trainer, McDougall, J. Jackson and McPherson. **Front row, left to right:** Edmed, Cyril Done, Morrison, Smith, Lucas and Hopkin.

Known as Jim "Parson" Jackson, this versatile and gritty full-back (pictured bottom left) invested his earnings playing football to study first at Liverpool University and then Cambridge, where he read Greek and Philosophy. In the summer of 1933 he was ordained as a Presbyterian minister, at which time he left the game to take up the Church full time.

Liverpool Pull Through in Extra Period

FINE RECOVERY

By BARRY THOMAS

Liverpool staged one of the most dramatic recoveries ever seen in a Cup-tie when they won their replay in extra time at Fulham yesterday by 5—2.

After an hour's play Fulham were leading 2—0 against a team shattered and disheartened. Defeat stared the Liverpool men in the face.

But with half an hour to go a goal was scored which turned the match round with a suddenness which simply amazed the spectators.

The ease with which Fulham had taken the lead and held it had lured them into a feeling of security, and defenders were standing still when a stray ball was dropped into the Fulham goalmouth.

Hanson, completely unmarked, trapped it, and, with seconds to spare, kicked it past Tootill into the net.

From that moment Liverpool realised they had a chance, and in their feverish efforts to draw level they found the team understanding which they had lacked for months.

BOTH TEAMS PLAYED OUT

Combination among the forwards reappeared. Hanson made several brilliant shots. And eventually, two minutes from normal full time, Bradshaw drove the ball thirty-five yards through the tricky wind, low into the corner obviously played out—Fulham in getting their lead and Liverpool by their mighty efforts to equalise. But whereas Liverpool were still playing methodically, Fulham's system had gone completely to pieces.

A second replay looked fairly certain until a few minutes from the end, when Roberts seised on a particularly brilliant short pass from Wright and drove the ball into the net.

Fulham flung the match away. In the first half their football was exhilarating. Gibbons held the middle of the Liverpool attack with ease, and Hammond was continually finding gaps for his passes out to Finch and Arnold.

SCOTT SAVES THE DAY

But Gibbons was exhausted long before the end. After the unexpected blow of Liverpool's first goal the fine receptive movements of the Fulham forwards were conspicuously absent.

Liverpool are to be highly praised for a victory nothing less than sensational, and for their courage in going all out for it. They had many disappointing players, however.

Scott, their veteran goalkeeper, was their hero, saving several shots in his old miraculous fashion, while Steele played solidly.

The star forward was Hanson, the outside left, who was always causing trouble in the great period of recovery by closing in for some really brilliant shooting.

Liverpool now meet Tranmere Rovers in the fourth round—at Liverpool, by arrangement. A crowd of 28,849 watched the game, the receipts being £1,897.

MR. BETTINSON'S PLANS

Wrestling Not a New Departure for N.S.C. - An Echo of 1909

Mr. Lionel Bettinson, the manager of the National Sporting Club, was at the Stadium Club, London, last night, to see a programme of "free style" wrestling.

The N.S.C. intend to stage a complete programme of wrestling at Olympia on January 26.

Mr. Bettinson said : "The National Sporting Club are by no means embarking on a departure in running wrestling shows. As far back as 1909 my father, Peggy Bettinson, ran wrestling shows at the Alhambra Theatre, Leicester-square, and they paid handsomely.

"At the old club premises in Covent Garden before that wrestling matches had been a feature."

AT HUDDERSFIELD

Where Huddersfield were obviously better was in the quickness and accuracy of their short passing game in their approach to goal. Usually the Argyle backs were unable to cope with the quick work of the Huddersfield forwards.

There was an high average level of merit in the Huddersfield team, but Goodall, Whittingham, young Mangnall, Luke and Holt may be singled out for special mention.

Apart from Briggs, Argyle, in the first half, put in few shots and their defence were inclined to impede each other.

Argyle had an early shock when Huddersfield scored through Luke. Within thirty seconds Mangnall increased the lead before the interval, and Huddersfield's second half goals were obtained by Holt, McLean and Mangnall (two).

Briggs scored for Argyle just before the interval and again near the finish.

The attendance was 13,507, and the receipts

Hammond scores Fulham's first goal against Liverpool.

Liverpool football team pose for a group photograph during their tour of the Balkans, on 12 June 1939. **Back row, left to right:** trainer Chas Wilson, Matt Busby, Ben Dabbs, Nivvy, Ted Savage, Hobson, Syd Roberts, Norman Low and Tommy Bradshaw. **Front row, left to right:** Eastham, Blenkinsop, Howe, Alf Hanson and Phil Taylor.

Liverpool team in the 1930s on a tour of Spain.

Matt Busby was captain of Liverpool in the late 1930s and a great friend of fellow Scot Bill Shankly. Although the onset of the Second World War cut short his Liverpool playing career he was so highly rated he was offered a coaching position immediately after the war. At the same time Manchester United offered him the position of manager, and after much soul searching he moved to Old Trafford. Long after he left Anfield Liverpool supporters still admired Busby for his playing days at Anfield. In 1966 a poll by readers of the *Kop* magazine, voted him as captain of a team of all-time Anfield greats.

–LEGENDS–

Gordon Hodgson

Born in South Africa to English parents, Gordon Hodgson was a talented all-round sportsman who played first-class cricket for Lancashire and also excelled at baseball. He caught the eye of Liverpool scouts when playing for a South African touring side, and signed professional terms with Liverpool in December 1925.

He was an energetic, robust, prolific marksman. He soon established himself as a goalscoring sensation in the First Division and set a new club record of 36 goals in one season, a record that stood until the emergence of Roger Hunt in the 1960s. He still holds the record of 17 hat-tricks during his spell at Liverpool. He was transferred to Aston Villa for £3,000 in 1936 and later became manager of Port Vale.

FOOTBALL
–STATS–

Gordon Hodgson

Name: Gordon Hodgson

Born: South Africa 1904

Died: Stoke-on-Trent 1951

Position: Inside centre-forward

Liverpool Playing Career: 1925-1936

Club Appearances: 378

Goals: 240

England Appearances: 3

Goals 1

Post War Glory, Then the Wilderness Years

1946-1959

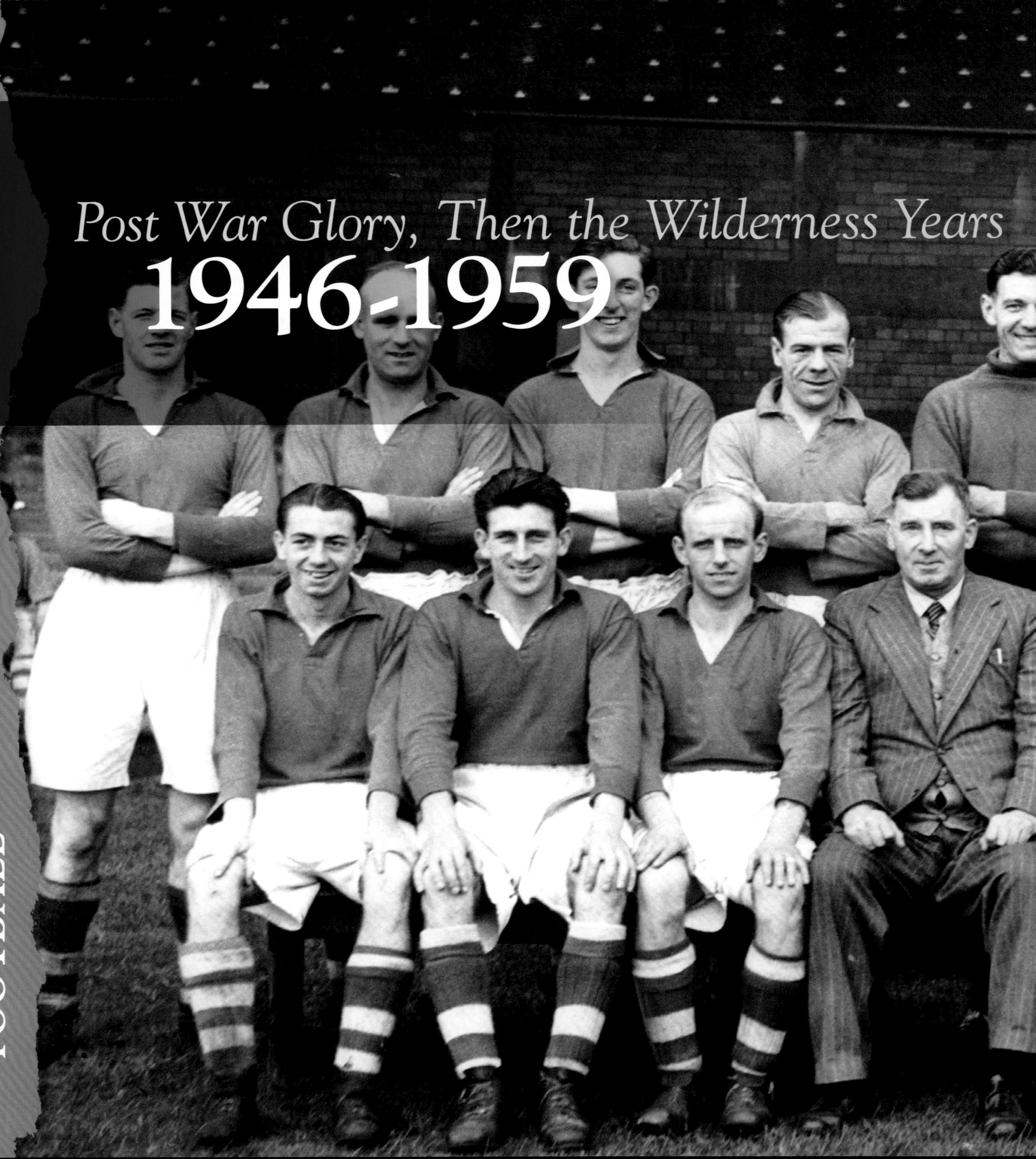

Liverpool FC, in October 1948. Back row, left to right: Eddie Spicer, Ray Lambert, Laurie Hughes, Bill Shepherd, Cyril Sidlow, Bill Jones, Phil Taylor, Bill Fagan, Ken Brierley, Albert Shelly (trainer). Front row, left to right: Jimmy Payne, Bill Watkinson, Doug McAvoy, George Kay (manager), Councillor S. Ronald Williams (chairman), Jack Balmer (captain), Cyril Done, Bob Paisley.

Liverpool goalkeeper Cyril Sidlow (seated) and Ray Lambert answer the urgent calls of their fans for last-minute autographs before the train draws out of Lime Street Station on the way to Wembley for the FA Cup final, 27 April 1950.

Daily Mirror April 29 1950 Page 10.

Police on duty outside Maine Road, Manchester, a few hours before the FA Cup semi-final between Liverpool and Everton 1950. Liverpool won the match 2-0 with goals from Paisley and Liddell to reach their second ever FA Cup final.

Liverpool manager George Kay led Liverpool to the First Division title in 1946-7 and the final of the FA Cup in 1950. He was a good motivator and a deep thinker. He was always smartly dressed and never wore a tracksuit, preferring to wear a suit and tie. He famously dropped Bob Paisley for the 1950 Cup final even though he had scored in the semi-final and his name was printed in the Cup final programme. He retired in 1951 due to ill health. Billy Liddell said of him *"if ever a man gave his life for a club, George Kay did so for Liverpool."*

THE FOOTBALL ASSOCIATION CHALLENGE CUP COMPETITION

FINAL TIE

Arsenal v Liverpool

SATURDAY, APRIL 29th, 1950 at 3 pm

OFFICIAL PROGRAMME - ONE SHILLING

The Empire Stadium

WEMBLEY

Chairman and Managing Director:
SIR ARTHUR J. ELVIN, MBE

The crowd at the scoreboard end in the 1950 FA Cup final between Arsenal and Liverpool. It was a very wet day at the Cup final, and these were the days before Wembley had a roof. Some had the foresight to bring umbrellas.

The Liverpool team posing for a group photograph before the League division match against Wolves at Anfield in 1950. **Back row, left to right:** Phil Taylor, Bill Jones, Ray Lambert, Cyril Sidlow, Bob Paisley and Eddie Spicer.
Front Row, left to right: Jimmy Payne, Kevin Baron, Albert Stubbins, Willie Fagan, Billy Liddell.

Bob Paisley, 1950.
He was left out for the final.

Despite defeat cheering crowds line the streets of Liverpool city centre as the Liverpool team is welcomed home at Lime Street the day after the 1950 Cup final.

–LEGENDS–

Albert Stubbins

Albert Stubbins was a powerful centre-forward with terrific pace and a fearsome right footed shot. Stubbins was already a legend on Tyneside for his goalscoring feats with Newcastle United during the Second World War, scoring 231 times in 188 appearances. He was undoubtedly one of the most popular players ever to wear the famous red shirt after having signed for a club record fee of £12,500 in September 1946, especially as he chose to sign for Liverpool ahead of Everton. He scored on his debut and was leading scorer with Liverpool in the first two seasons after the war.

He was kept out of the England line-up only by the brilliant Tommy Lawton, although he did play for the Football League on several occasions. A gentleman on and off the field, Stubbins was nicknamed "the smiling assassin" and famously appeared on the cover of The Beatles album *Sgt Peppers Lonely Hearts Club Band*.

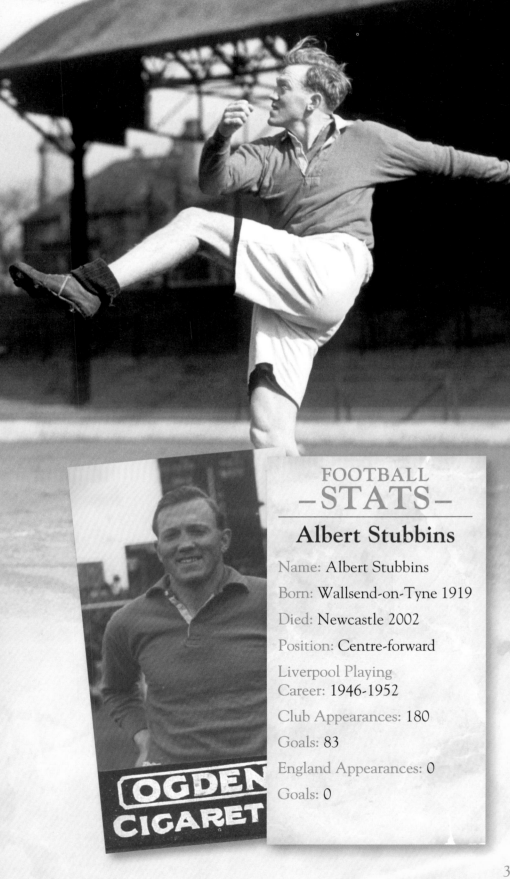

FOOTBALL –STATS–

Albert Stubbins

Name: Albert Stubbins

Born: Wallsend-on-Tyne 1919

Died: Newcastle 2002

Position: Centre-forward

Liverpool Playing Career: 1946-1952

Club Appearances: 180

Goals: 83

England Appearances: 0

Goals: 0

Huddersfield v Liverpool 1950

Division One match at Leeds Road, 11 November 1950: Huddersfield Town 2 v Liverpool 2. Liverpool players Bill Jones and Bob Paisley challenge Huddersfield forwards Jimmy Glazzard and Albert Nightingale during the match.

English League Division One match, 9 December 1950: Portsmouth 1 v Liverpool 3. Action during the match as Jimmy Payne (7) watches the ball go into the net for a Liverpool goal.

Action from the Norwich v Liverpool FA Cup third round tie on 6 January 1951. Liverpool lost 3-1. Here we see Liverpool on the attack with Hughes (left) Stubbins (centre) and Payne on the floor near the goalpost.

Phil Taylor, Liverpool captain, followed by Bob Paisley, in 1950. Phil Taylor went on to manage Liverpool from 1956 to 1959.

Liverpool's goalkeeper Russell Crossley clears the ball in the
Cup defeat against Norwich, in 1951.

Jimmy Seddon, Liverpool trainer and "magic" spongeman, 1953.

Fulham v Liverpool at Craven Cottage, 1952.

Liverpool manager Don Welsh explains tactics to a young boy. Unfortunately for Welsh, he was the first manager to take Liverpool down to the Second Division in over 50 years in the 1953-4 season. On the same day Everton were promoted back to the First Division. Liverpool would stay in the Second Division for eight seasons with only the chance of FA Cup success to keep the fans hopeful. They nearly returned to the First Division in 1955-6, narrowly missing out coming third (when only the top two were promoted). Welsh wasn't given another chance at promotion and he became the first Liverpool manager ever to be sacked. Ex-player and captain Phil Taylor who had joined the backroom staff after retiring when Liverpool were relegated, succeeded Don Welsh.

Liverpool v Barnsley at Anfield, 10 December 1955. Ronnie Moran of Liverpool (with Geoff Twentyman in the background) and Brown of Barnsley go for the ball.

–LEGENDS–

Billy Liddell

Billy Liddell was a true Anfield great. He signed for Liverpool in June 1938 after being recommended by Liverpool captain Matt Busby. During the Second World War Liddell served in the RAF but returned to pick up a championship medal in the 1946-7 season and played in the 1950 Cup final. Liddell played at Wembley against Arsenal but was injured in the early stages of the game and limped around for most of the match as substitutes were not allowed in those days. Although he was primarily a left-winger he was so versatile that he could play on the right wing or as a centre-forward. In fact he was such a utility player he played in many positions. When he was in his prime Liverpool were relegated to the Second Division and Liddell terrorized defences there, scoring 30 goals in 40 matches during the 1954-5 season; but he couldn't help them to get promotion during the 1950s. He won 28 Scotland caps and scored on his debut against England at Hampden Park.

Trainer and coach Bob Paisley of Liverpool on the left putting some of the team members through heading practice at Liverpool's training ground, at Melwood, August 1956. **Left to right:** Geoff Twentyman, John Evans, Tommy Younger, Billy Liddell and Laurie Hughes.

Billy Liddell challenges Sheffield United's goalkeeper Alan Hodgkinson, April 1958.

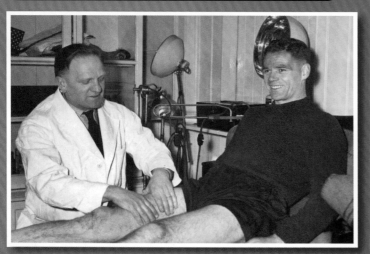

Treatment table 1950s style. Liverpool trainer Albert Shelley gives Billy Liddell a massage, 1958.

Billy Liddell at his testimonial in 1960 at Anfield followed by Tom Finney and legendary goalkeeper Bert Trautmann.

FOOTBALL
–STATS–

Billy Liddell

Name: William Beveridge Liddell

Born: Dunfermline 1922

Died: Liverpool 2001

Position: Outside-left, Centre-forward

Liverpool Playing Career: 1939-1960

Club Appearances: 537

Goals: 229

Scotland Appearances: 28

Goals: 6

A Liverpool defender clears the ball v Southend in the FA Cup third round January 1958.

Liverpool fans congratulate Billy Liddell after beating Southend United 3-2 in the FA Cup third round replay in January 1958. But the fans' celebrations would be short lived as the team went out in the sixth round to Blackburn.

Liverpool's FA Cup nightmare continued when they lost to non-League Worcester City. Billy Liddell was dropped for the first time in his career for this match and helped the trainer Albert Shelley put studs in the boots of the other players.

Liverpool goalkeeper Tommy Younger picks himself up from the back of the net after failing to judge a shot from Gosling of Worcester, for their second goal, 15 January 1959.

Above: The Corinthian Spirit. Liverpool goalkeeper Tommy Younger (left) congratulates Worcester goalscorers Bernie Gosling (centre) and Tommy Skuse (right) in their dressing room after the match, 15 January 1959.

Left: FA Cup fourth round at St George's Lane. Worcester City 2 v Liverpool 1, 15 January 1959. Worcester goalkeeper Kirkwood comes out to save the ball from Liverpool outside-right Morris as defenders look on.

The Messiah Arrives: The Bill Shankly Era
1959-1974

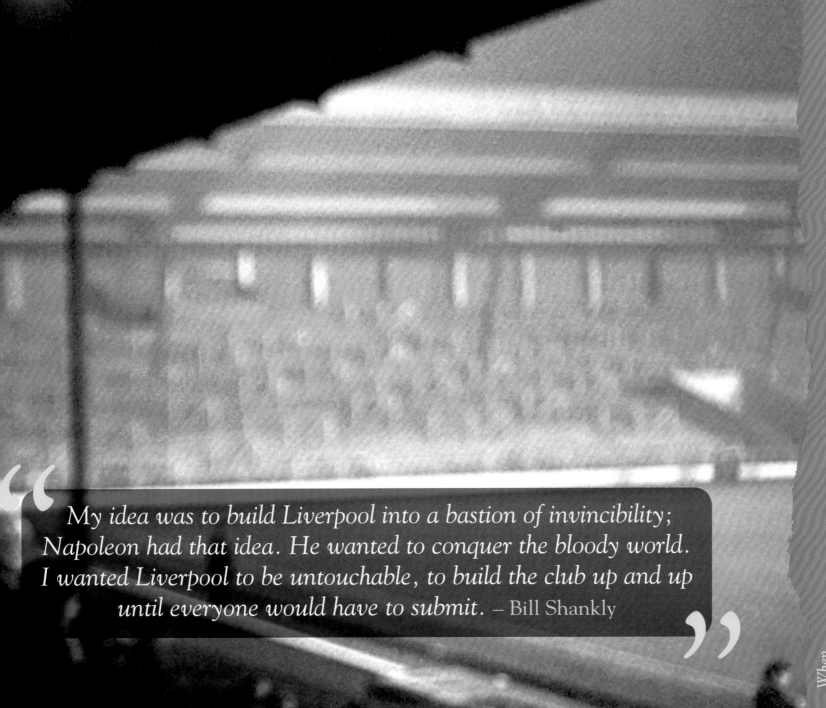

" *My idea was to build Liverpool into a bastion of invincibility; Napoleon had that idea. He wanted to conquer the bloody world. I wanted Liverpool to be untouchable, to build the club up and up until everyone would have to submit.* – Bill Shankly "

Born in the coalmining village of Glenbuck, Ayrshire, in September 1913, Bill Shankly transformed Liverpool Football Club with a combination of natural enthusiasm, vision and inspirational leadership. He was a true "man of the people" and football was his passion. The humble surroundings of the close-knit coalmining village had shaped Shankly's character, and football was in his blood. Two of his uncles played for clubs and his four brothers played professionally also. Bill Shankly was spotted as a promising young player by Carlisle United scouts and signed for them in 1932 at the age of 18. After playing only a handful of games for the Third Division club the promising young Scotsman was snapped up by Second Division Preston North End for a fee of £500. It was at Preston that Shankly fulfilled his potential as a player, helping them gain promotion to the First Division and winning 12 caps for Scotland. It is widely acknowledged that his years at Preston finely tuned his footballing philosophy that would eventually turn him into a legend at Anfield.

Preston North End FA Cup winners 1938. Shankly (back row, far left), Gallimore, Scott (trainer), Holdcroft, Beattie, Batey, Maxwell, Beattie, Mutch, Smith (captain), Watmough, O'Donnell.

Shankly was the manager of Huddersfield at this time. Shankly had joined the Yorkshire club in December 1955 after previously managing Workington Town. Like Liverpool, Huddersfield languished in the Second Division. Shankly had tried to improve the Huddersfield team and had actually enquired about buying Ian St John and Ron Yeats, but Huddersfield didn't have sufficient funds. Denis Law also played for Huddersfield, as did future England and Everton full-back Ray Wilson. The course of football history may well have been changed if the Huddersfield Board had come up with the money!

Bill Shankly (right) when manager of Carlisle in 1951 talking to his players including Geoff Twentyman (centre), who later played for Liverpool and then became a very successful scout for the club.

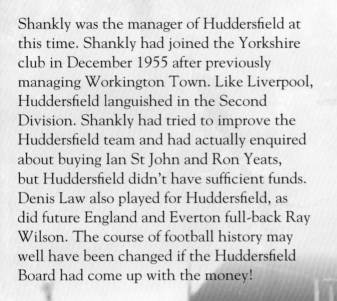

Bill Shankly (left) with brother Bob, manager of Third Lanark FC of Glasgow, inspecting the team shirts in 1958.

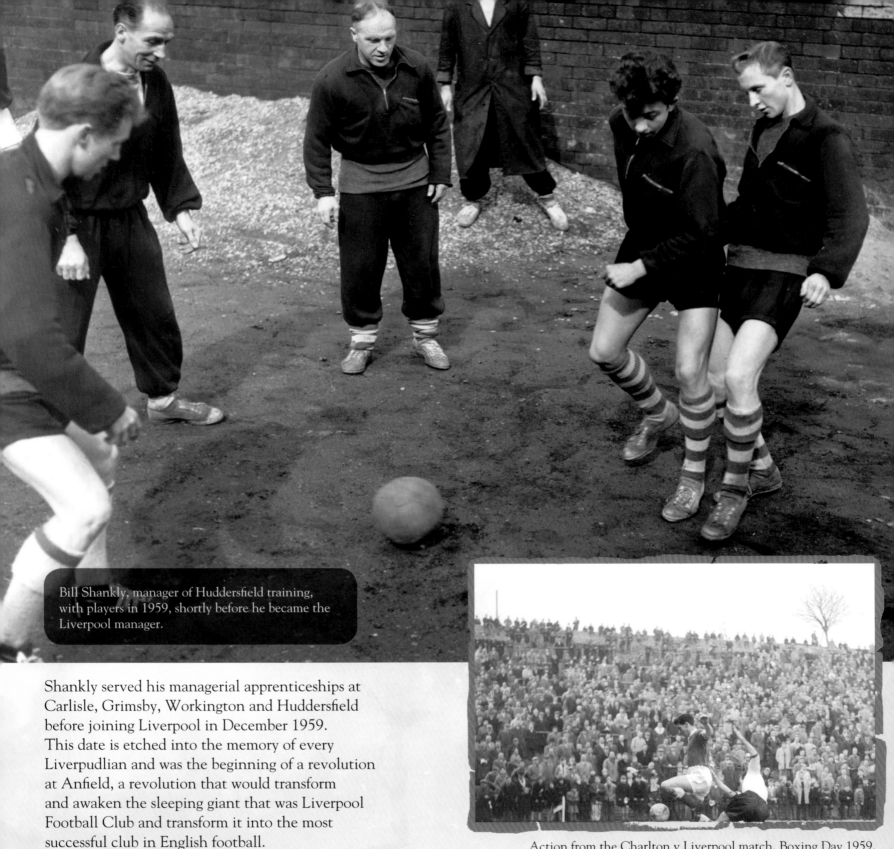

Shankly served his managerial apprenticeships at Carlisle, Grimsby, Workington and Huddersfield before joining Liverpool in December 1959. This date is etched into the memory of every Liverpudlian and was the beginning of a revolution at Anfield, a revolution that would transform and awaken the sleeping giant that was Liverpool Football Club and transform it into the most successful club in English football.

Action from the Charlton v Liverpool match, Boxing Day 1959.

Action from the Liverpool v Manchester United FA Cup fourth round tie at Anfield, January 1960. Liverpool lost 3-1.

Liverpool goalkeeper Tommy Younger scrambles in the mud for the ball as Ronnie Moran (left) and Dick White look on as a Charlton forward closes in.

Shortly after Bill Shankly became manager Liverpool lost their first run of matches. He knew he had a lot of rebuilding to do. Liverpool lost this match 3-0 away to Charlton Athletic on Boxing Day December 1959.

> "At a football club there is a holy trinity – the players, the manager and the supporters. Directors don't come into it. They are only there to sign the cheques." – Bill Shankly

The Board of Directors at Liverpool FC in the early 1960s. **Left to right:** S C Reakes, C J Hill, H Cartwright, G A Richards, R L Martindale, T V Williams (chairman) J S McInnes (secretary), Bill Shankly (manager), E A F Sawyer, H K Latham.

Bill Shankly the "Messiah" arrived at Anfield to succeed manager Phil Taylor, who had left the club by mutual agreement. Taylor had resigned tired and exhausted from his attempts to gain Liverpool promotion from the Second Division to the top flight. Bill Shankly could have arrived at Liverpool some eight years earlier – he had been offered the post in 1951 but refused at that time because in those days the manager did not pick the team. That was the preserve of a committee of club directors and executives. In 1959 Liverpool's chairman, T V Williams, approached Bill Shankly when he was the manager at Huddersfield. Shankly had become frustrated at Huddersfield as he wanted to buy new players and improve the team but no transfer money was forthcoming. Shankly was impressed by Williams's forthright approach and although they didn't always see eye to eye with him the partnership worked. Shankly knew that Williams had a lot of power in the Liverpool Boardroom and Shankly actually nicknamed him "De Gaulle" because he reminded him of the French leader in the Second World War. When the charismatic Shankly arrived at Anfield he was the first manager to pick the team and identify transfer targets, conditions that he had insisted upon before he accepted the post.

When he arrived at Anfield Shankly famously called the ground the "biggest slum in Liverpool". It was dilapidated and needed renovating; the training ground was big enough but needed improving as well, and then there was the team! From the outset he went about assessing the players, the staff and the directors to see what was needed. He didn't bring his own staff in, as many managers do, but he called a meeting and asked backroom staff such as Bob Paisley, Joe Fagan and Reuben Bennett to work in harmony with him.

Shankly then went about assessing the players. Gerry Byrne was transfer listed when he arrived, but was soon taken from the list, though Shankly did let 24 players go over the first few seasons. In 1959-60 and 1960-1 Liverpool finished third on both occasions, narrowly missing out on promotion. When Shankly arrived at Liverpool he knew they had little or no money, and it wasn't until a year and a half into his reign, when Eric Sawyer arrived in the Boardroom, that things began to change. Sawyer, who worked for the Littlewoods organization, became an ally of Shankly and shared his vision for the club. He told Shankly that "if you can get the players I can get the money". In the summer of 1961 Shankly got his players. He made two signings that were instrumental in the rejuvenation of Liverpool Football Club. They were Ian St John, an energetic centre-forward from Motherwell, and Ron Yeats, a dominating centre-half from Dundee United. According to Shankly they were his greatest signings and the dawning of a new age at Liverpool Football Club. These two players, together with goalkeeper Tommy Lawrence (who had come through the ranks at Anfield), would form the spine of the Liverpool team for nearly a decade and would help to transform fortunes on the pitch and lay the foundations for Liverpool's dominance in the 1970s and '80s.

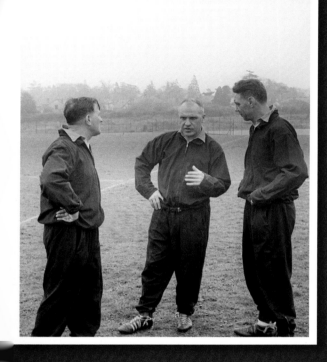

Above: Gerry Byrne at Anfield 1959.

Top Left: Bill Shankly talks to backroom staff Bob Paisley (left) and Joe Fagan (right).

Left: Bill Shankly in his office with his famous typewriter.

Bill Shankly read in the papers that Motherwell had put St John up for sale. Shankly told the Board that he wanted to buy him but one of the directors said "We can't afford to sign him". One of the directors, Eric Sawyer, replied "We can't afford not to sign him". Shankly got his wish and soon St John was playing for the Reds.

Right: Ian St John in action against West Ham, 1962.

Motherwell football player Ian St John jumps for the ball against Kilmarnock in Scottish League First Division match, February 1960.

Ron Yeats arrived at Anfield from Dundee United in the summer of 1961 for £30,000. Shankly told reporters *"He's a colossus. Come outside and I'll give you a walk around him"*. Immediately appointed captain, Yeats led the new look Liverpool to promotion as Second Division champions (1961-2) in his first season.

Ron Yeats in action at Anfield.

The 1962-3 season in the First Division was a period of consolidation and strengthening, and Liverpool finished a respectable eighth in the League. Shankly added more pieces to the jigsaw by buying wing-half Willie Stevenson from Glasgow Rangers for the bargain price of £7,000 and stylish left-winger Peter Thompson from Preston for £40,000.

Above: The newly promoted Liverpool team pose for a group photograph at their training ground, 15 August 1962. **Back row, left to right:** Gordon Milne, Gerry Byrne, Tommy Leishman, Jim Furnell, Tommy Lawrence, Ron Yeats, and Ronnie Moran. **Centre row, left to right:** Kevin Lewis, Roger Hunt, Ian St John, Jimmy Melia, and Alan A'Court. **Front row, left to right:** Alan Jones, Alfie Arrowsmith, Johnny Morrissey and Ian Callaghan.

Right: Fancy dress was not on the agenda in those days. Christmas parties were so different then! Here we see Liverpool players enjoying their Christmas party in 1962.

Ian St John celebrates the third goal against Burnley at Turf Moor, which put Liverpool on their way to their first title since 1946-7. Ian St John scored 21 goals in that title-winning season.

Left: An injured Roger Hunt pours the tea for team-mates Ron Yeats (centre) Alf Arrowsmith (left) and Willie Stevenson (right) after the match.

Right: Liverpool's left-back Ronnie Moran in action against Spurs, watched by Ian St John, March 1964. Liverpool beat Spurs 3-1 at Anfield on their way to winning the League.

Liverpool League Champions 1963-4. The Liverpool team celebrate from the directors' box with an imitation cup, April 1964. **Left to right:** St John. Milne, Thompson, Callaghan, Arrowsmith, Bill Shankly (manager), Ron Yeats (captain), Lawrence, Byrne, Hunt and Stevenson.

Liverpool FC was rising from its slumber, and despite losing their first three home games in the 1963-4 season they swept to their first title since 1946-7 with three games to spare by thrashing Arsenal 5-0 at Anfield. Yet they were not awarded the actual trophy on that

Ian St John scores the first in a 5-0 victory over Arsenal, which secured Liverpool the title.

day: Football League protocol would not allow them to have the trophy until the season was over and as Liverpool won the League with three games left they had to make do with a papier-mâché trophy.

Liverpool players celebrate in the dressing room.

Roger Hunt was besieged by autograph hunters at Anfield, on Boxing Day 1963: Liverpool had just beaten Stoke City 6-1. Hunt netted four that day and went on to score 31 in the League, which swept Liverpool to their first title since 1947.

Jimmy Melia was a stalwart of the Liverpool side from the mid-1950s. He was a hard working inside forward with a football brain. We can see him here soaking his feet in a warm bucket of water, after a long hard season – this was treatment 1960s style! Liverpool had been promoted and the 1962-3 season was the first in the top flight since their relegation in 1954. Melia played a big part in the campaign of 1961-2 and was an ever present when they won promotion. He played 39 games in the 1962-3 season before drifting out of the reckoning and being sold to Wolves for £55,000 in March 1964.

Peter Thompson buys bacon at the local shop for his landlady, April 1964. His speed, skill and ability to deliver superb crosses helped Liverpool become a force at home and abroad during the 1960s.

Liverpool's strike force had been prolific in the 1963-4 season. Strikers Roger Hunt, Ian St John and Alf Arrowsmith had scored 67 of Liverpool's 97 League goals, many supplied by right-winger Ian Callaghan and Peter Thompson on the left wing.

Even Dixie Dean, the legendary Everton goalscorer, commented that he would have liked to have played between that pair of wingers.

Ian Callaghan, the ever dependable right-winger who played 843 games for Liverpool between 1959 and 1978. He was the only Liverpool player whose career spanned the Reds' rise from the doldrums of the Second Division to the triumphs of League Titles, FA Cup wins and European glory.

Peter Thompson in action against Derby, November 1969, at the Baseball Ground.

Liverpool players ordering food in a deli near their hotel in New York City, May 1964. **Left to right:** Ronnie Moran, Ian Callaghan, Gerry Byrne and Alan A'Court.

After winning the championship Liverpool players are seen here sightseeing in New York, in front of the Empire State Building, 19 May 1964. **Left to right:** Alan A'Court, Ian Callaghan, Ronnie Moran and Gerry Byrne. They were on a goodwill tour in conjunction with the American Soccer League.

TRAYS
SILVERWARE
and NAPKINS
SERVED at COUNTER

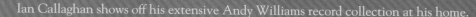

Cilla Black with Bill Shankly at Melwood, Liverpool's training ground. Shankly knew the importance of show business in popular culture and he was happy to be photographed with Liverpool stars.

Liverpool FC's rise as a force in the game coincided with the "Swinging Sixties". Liverpool seemed to be the centre of the cultural universe as Beatlemania and the Merseybeat groups conquered the charts at home and abroad. The Spion Kop at Anfield was also becoming famous as Liverpool fans adopted many of the songs popularized by Merseybeat groups. A BBC documentary team were dispatched to Anfield to document this new phenomenon and were bewildered at the passion and ferocity of the crowd who sang versions of *She Loves You* by The Beatles, *Anyone Who Had A Heart* by Cilla Black and an adaptation of The Routers' *Lets Go* in tribute to their idol St John. However, it was one song in particular that had become an anthem for Liverpool fans: *You'll Never Walk Alone*. When Gerry and the Pacemakers recorded this track from the Rodgers and Hammerstein musical *Carousel*, it became Number One in the charts for four weeks in late 1963 and was played as the final record before the teams came on to the pitch. The Kop sang along with it and even when it dropped out of the charts they continued to sing it and a football anthem was born. At the same time, Liverpool entertainers and comedians were also becoming household names, and no photo opportunity was lost.

Ian St John, Ron Yeats, Ken Dodd, and Billy Liddell posing as The Beatles, 1963.

Ken Dodd training with Liverpool. On the eve of the FA Cup final in 1965 the team went to see the Liverpool comedian on stage at the London Palladium as a way of relaxing.

Bill Shankly signing autographs.

Bill Shankly was a genuine "man of the people" and he would often go into the community to watch matches. Here we see him watching a match from a flat above Eldon Grove, just off Liverpool's Scotland Road. Bill travelled down to watch the kids play on a dull drizzly night, and after the Scotty Road team had beaten a team from Everton 7-1, Bill had a cup of tea with the lads. He commented *"it's not like Cologne or Brussels but then there's no place like Eldon Grove"*.

Ron Yeats and Bobby Moore after Charity Shield match at Anfield, August 1964.
Liverpool, the League Champions, shared the trophy with FA Cup winners West Ham
after a 2-2 draw.

Hammers fan "Alf Garnett" in an episode of the popular BBC TV comedy *Till Death Us Do Part*, being filmed at Anfield.

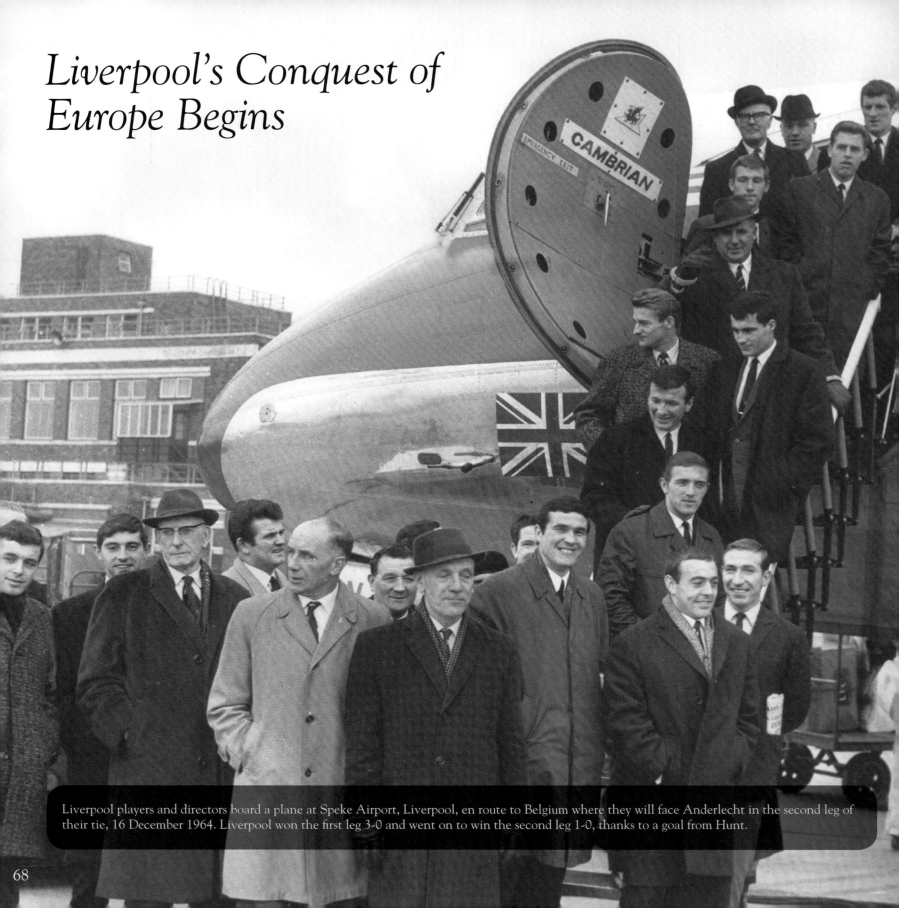

Liverpool's Conquest of Europe Begins

Liverpool players and directors board a plane at Speke Airport, Liverpool, en route to Belgium where they will face Anderlecht in the second leg of their tie, 16 December 1964. Liverpool won the first leg 3-0 and went on to win the second leg 1-0, thanks to a goal from Hunt.

Chris Lawler, an ever dependable right-back, played 549 games for Liverpool scoring an impressive 61 goals. He played in both of Shankly's title-winning teams of the 1960s and 1970s.

Liverpool goalkeeper Tommy Lawrence dives at the feet of George Best in front of the Stretford End goal prior to the roof being put on the Scoreboard End at Old Trafford in the background.

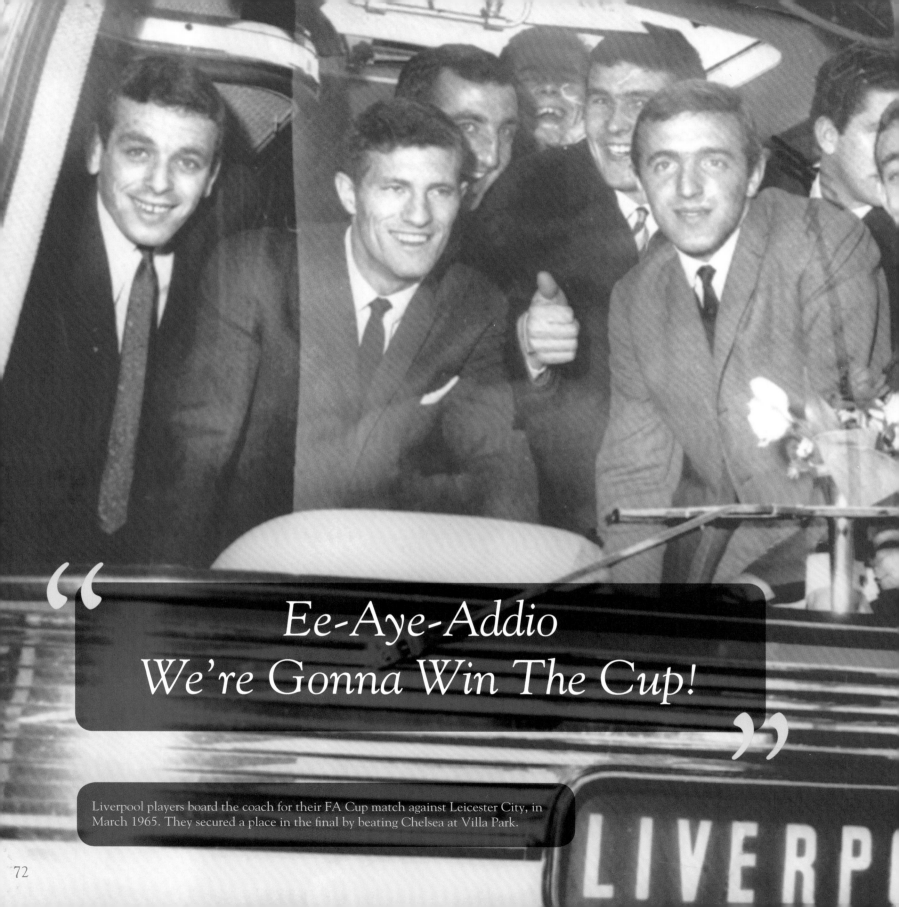

> ## Ee-Aye-Addio
> ## We're Gonna Win The Cup!

Liverpool players board the coach for their FA Cup match against Leicester City, in March 1965. They secured a place in the final by beating Chelsea at Villa Park.

Bill Shankly and Tommy Docherty. When they met as opposing managers of Liverpool and Chelsea in the FA Cup semi-final at Villa Park in April 1965, Shankly said to Docherty *"Tom, I think your team's good enough to win the Cup... next year!"*

The year after Shankly had delivered the League championship he achieved something that no other manager had achieved in 73 years of trying: he led Liverpool FC to FA Cup glory. Beaten semi-finalists on several occasions and finalists in 1914 and 1950, this was Liverpool Football Club's "Holy Grail". Many Liverpool fans had thought they would never see the day when Liverpool won at Wembley to lift the Cup.

The success had not been without its setbacks though, with Liverpool drawing at home to Stockport County then languishing at the bottom of the Fourth Division and going to a replay against their "bogey" team of the time, Leicester City.

Fans at Villa Park 1965, Liverpool v Chelsea.

Peter Thompson beats Peter "the Cat" Bonetti with a tremendous shot to score Liverpool's first goal at Villa Park against Chelsea as Roger Hunt looks on.

Left: Liverpool fans celebrate on the pitch after beating Chelsea 2-0 at Villa Park in the FA Cup semi-final.

Below: The Liverpool team celebrate with directors after Liverpool had just beaten Chelsea in the semi-final of the FA Cup, reaching their first final since 1950.

Liverpool FC April 1965.

Liverpool FC team photographed here in their all red strip which had first been worn against Anderlecht in the European Cup earlier in the 1964-5 season. Shankly thought the team would look bigger and more formidable in all red. When he first saw Ron Yeats in the new kit he said *"Jesus Christ son, you look eight feet tall"*.

Gerry Byrne, Ian Callaghan, Gordon Milne, Roger Hunt and Ronnie Moran head for Wembley from Lime Street to play Leeds in the FA Cup final, April 1965.

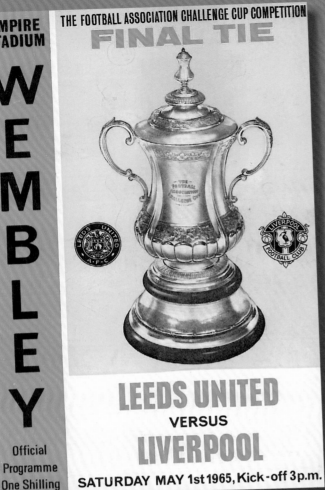

FA Cup final, Wembley, 1 May 1965. Liverpool beat Leeds United 2-1. Tommy Smith of Liverpool tackles Norman Hunter of Leeds.

Ian St John and Ron Yeats: Liverpool keep close to Billy Bremner of Leeds.

Team caricatures in the *Daily Mirror* on the morning of the FA Cup final.

Bill Shankly celebrates at Wembley with his "colossus" Ron Yeats.

Liverpool celebrate winning the FA Cup. **Left to right:** Stevenson, Yeats, Lawler, Hunt, Thompson, Byrne, Smith and Strong.

Massive crowds welcomed home Liverpool players after their FA Cup win.

80

The Liverpool team parade the FA Cup through a packed Liverpool city centre. After 73 years and 207 ties Liverpool had finally won the Cup!

Liverpool Play Inter Milan in European Cup Semi-final, 4 May 1965

Gerry Byrne (left) and Gordon Milne parade the FA Cup around Anfield before the European Cup semi-final against Inter Milan three days after the victory at Wembley. Gerry Byrne achieved hero status with Liverpool fans by playing through the FA Cup final with Leeds with a broken collar bone.

In those days substitutes were not allowed and Byrne played through the pain barrier producing one of the most courageous Wembley performances of all time, even setting up Roger Hunt's goal which put Liverpool ahead in extra time. Shankly even suggested that Byrne should have received all 11 FA Cup winners' medals, such was his courage that day. Gordon Milne had been ruled out of both games with a knee injury.

Shankly: *"For a player to be good enough to play for Liverpool, he must be prepared to run through a brick wall for me and then come out fighting on the other side."* In the FA Cup final Gerry Byrne did just that, epitomizing Shankly's philosophy on football.

" *Oh, Inter, one-two-three. Go back to Italy.*
(The Kop sang this to the tune of Santa Lucia). "

The gates for this match were locked two hours before the kick-off. The crowd was described as the noisiest and most passionate ever gathered inside a British stadium. When Byrne and Milne paraded the Cup around the ground the crowd went wild. The match itself has gone down in Liverpool folklore and is heralded as one of the great Anfield European nights. Liverpool scored after four minutes when Roger Hunt volleyed an Ian Callaghan cross into the net, but Inter soon hit back with an equalizer. Liverpool then went on to give Inter, the reigning world champions, a footballing lesson, totally outclassing them. Inter were managed by the great Argentinean coach and tactician Helenio Herrera who made famous the defensive system known as "catenaccio" (in Italian, meaning to bolt the door) a highly organized system designed to prevent goals. That night Liverpool demolished the Italians and could have scored 4 had a Chris Lawler goal five minutes before half-time not been controversially ruled offside. After Hunt's opener they went on to score another two goals by Callaghan and St John to give Liverpool a 3-1 lead going into the second leg at the San Siro. Herrera commented after the Anfield humiliation: "We have been beaten before, but tonight we were defeated." Everybody knew what he meant and Shankly thought that this was one of the greatest games he had ever seen – and most at Anfield that night agreed with him. Shankly knew that this Inter team was one of the best in the world and his Liverpool had absolutely destroyed them on that historic night.

Liverpool players celebrate as Hunt opens the scoring against Inter Milan.

Shirley Bassey is seen here giving a farewell song to the Liverpool squad on the evening of their departure to Milan for their European semi-final second leg. With Ron Yeats on piano, the team sang one of Shirley's numbers, *As Long As He Needs Me*, 10 May 1965. It was the calm before the storm.

If the Anfield leg was a nightmare for Inter then the return leg was even worse for Liverpool. Church bells near the hotel at Lake Como had kept Liverpool players awake the night before the game, and when they arrived at the San Siro the reception was poisonous. Smoke bombs, flares, coins and other objects rained down on to the pitch from the 90,000 crowd and the Liverpool players were abused and spat at. Shankly said it was "like a war" and that he had "never seen such hostility". Liverpool lost the match 3-0 and their chance to become the first British team to reach the European Cup final was over, after a series of controversial refereeing decisions. The memory of that night and especially the referee haunted Bill Shankly and his players for many years to come.

> "I don't believe in training twice a day. It does them no good at all. We train hard but sensibly. We train for football, little two minutes of torture, half a minute off, then on again. – Bill Shankly

Ian St John driving his newly purchased Ford Cortina to training in 1965.

Left: Liverpool players and staff report for pre-season training at Melwood as '60s tower blocks are constructed in the background.

Below: Willie Stevenson and Liverpool players training at Melwood, 1967. The famous "sweatbox" is in the background.

Left: Willie Stevenson, Ian St John and Ron Yeats share a joke in training.

Below: Liverpool FC treatment room, 1966. Legend has it that Bill Shankly ignored injured players but this photo seems to cast that theory into doubt.

Liverpool captain Ron Yeats and Celtic captain Billy McNeill shake hands before the first leg of the European Cup Winners Cup at Parkhead, 14 April 1966, in front of a crowd of 80,000.

St John's Ambulance men help clear up the bottles thrown on to the pitch. Some 50 people were injured.

The referee had to stop play as Liverpool goalkeeper Tommy Lawrence ran for safety. The police moved in to restore order and the referee was able to finish the match.

After the bottle party! Liverpool groundsman John Roberts lines up the bottles thrown on to the pitch the previous night. Bill Shankly famously asked Jock Stein if Celtic wanted their share of the gate receipts or just wanted the empties back.

Shankly was convinced Liverpool were the best team in Europe in the mid-1960s. He felt that his team had been cheated out of winning the European Cup two years before his great friend and Celtic manager Jock Stein led the "Lisbon Lions" to become the first British team to lift the trophy. This opinion was reinforced by Liverpool winning the First Division championship again in the 1965-6 season, using only 14 players all season and enjoying their best defensive record since the 1922-3 season. They also beat Celtic in the European Cup Winners Cup semi-final in April 1966. Celtic won the first leg 1-0 in Glasgow and they were in confident mood when they arrived at Anfield. Liverpool deservedly won the second leg 2-0 with goals from a Tommy Smith free kick and a Geoff Strong header. As the Kop erupted to celebrate Liverpool's first European final the mood at the other end of the ground turned ugly as Celtic fans rained beer bottles from the Anfield Road end towards Liverpool keeper Tommy Lawrence

League winners, 1966.

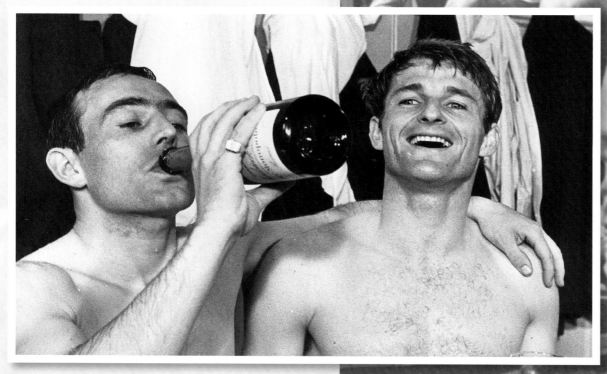

Ian St John and Roger Hunt celebrate winning the League,
April 1966. Hunt scored two second half goals against
Chelsea to clinch the title.

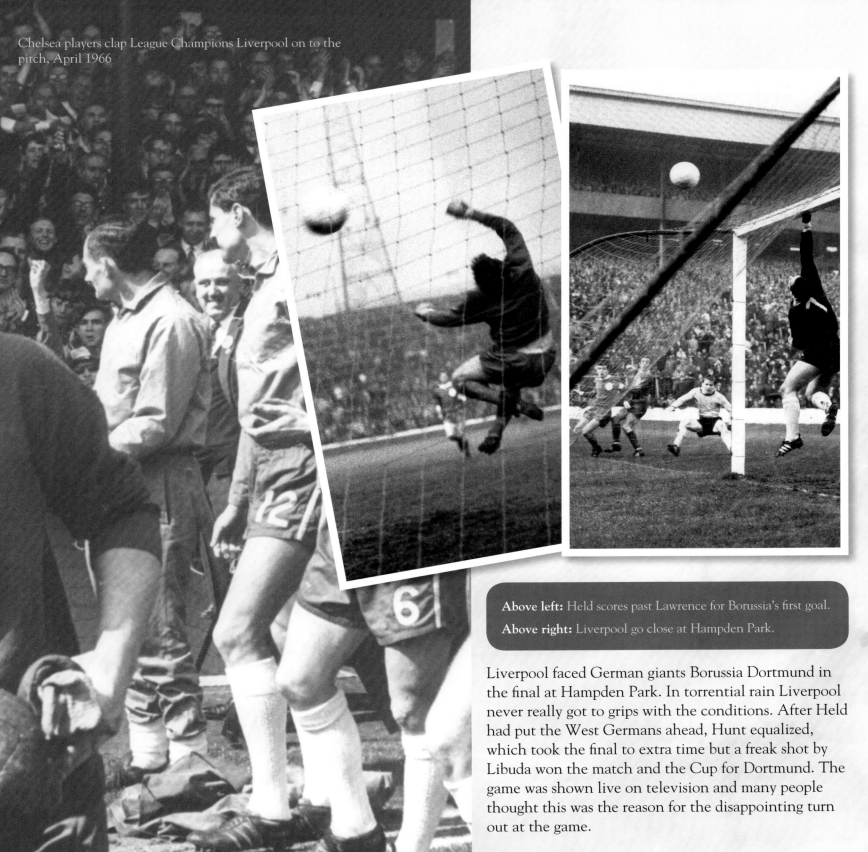

Chelsea players clap League Champions Liverpool on to the pitch, April 1966

Above left: Held scores past Lawrence for Borussia's first goal.

Above right: Liverpool go close at Hampden Park.

Liverpool faced German giants Borussia Dortmund in the final at Hampden Park. In torrential rain Liverpool never really got to grips with the conditions. After Held had put the West Germans ahead, Hunt equalized, which took the final to extra time but a freak shot by Libuda won the match and the Cup for Dortmund. The game was shown live on television and many people thought this was the reason for the disappointing turn out at the game.

Roger Hunt of Liverpool and England and Ray Wilson of Everton and England parade the World Cup before the 1966 Charity Shield at Goodison Park.

League, World Cup and FA Cup Trophies on display at Goodison Park, August 1966.

Ron Yeats of Liverpool is seen here displaying the League championship trophy and Brian Labone of Everton holds the FA Cup on a lap of honour before the Charity Shield match at Goodison Park 1966. Liverpool won the game 1-0 with a goal by Hunt. Watching from the Liverpool bench that day was a young 15-year-old boy called Kenny Dalglish, who was on trial at Anfield; but it would be another 11 years before the "lad with the golden hair" would sign for Liverpool and create history himself.

A young Johan Cruyff of Ajax scores past a diving Tommy Lawrence at Anfield, in December 1966, in the second leg of the European Cup tie.

The 1966-7 season was a major disappointment for Liverpool. Bill Shankly had been confident that the team could retain the championship but they struggled and could only manage fifth place. The team was showing signs of fatigue and the results reflected this. The FA Cup campaign was also a let down when Liverpool were put out of the competition at Goodison in the fifth round by their local rivals Everton, with a goal from Everton new boy Alan Ball.

The European campaign also stalled when the emerging Dutch masters Ajax beat Liverpool 7-3 on aggregate. A young unknown, Johan Cruyff, inspired the emerging Dutch side who beat Liverpool 5-1 in a foggy night in Amsterdam. Many thought the match should have been postponed as visibility was poor. Shankly talked up his team's chances in the second leg, but Ajax remained calm despite a Liverpool onslaught and came away with a 2-2 draw. This defeat hurt Shankly in particular and damaged Liverpool's hard-earned reputation in Europe.

Roger Hunt scores for Liverpool in the 2-2 draw against Ajax at Anfield in December 1966.

Daily Mirror

'Smoke bomb' haze starts surge forward

1 25

4d.   Thursday, December 15, 1966   No. 19,589

200 HURT IN SOCCER CRUSH AT BIG MATCH

By MIRROR REPORTER

TWO hundred people were hurt last night in thirty minutes of pandemonium at a football ground.

More than 20,000 fans watching a European Cup match from the "Spion Kop" end at Anfield, Liverpool, suddenly surged forward.

Thousands of spectators at the front fled, or were led away to save them from being crushed.

Thirty-one of the injured were taken to hospital. Eight were detained.

A near-maximum crowd of 52,000 were watching Liverpool play a Dutch team—Ajax of Amsterdam—when the trouble began.

At first it was thought that the "Kop" crowd surged forward because smoke bombs had been let off.

But later, Liverpool club secretary Peter Robinson said:

"The police now believe that perspiration in the crowd at the top caused the trouble.

"The perspiration formed into clouds of steam and rose from the crowd. People at the back couldn't see—so they pushed forward."

Bunched

Mr. Robinson added: "This sounds fantastic. But it has happened at big games at Liverpool before.

"The crowd are bunched together so tightly that their perspiration rises in steam."

Within seconds of the great surge forward, hundreds of men women and children were being carried, or were scrapping over the concrete barricades behind the goal.

Victims of the crush . . . young fans lie scattered near the Liverpool goal during the chaotic scenes at last night's match.

First-aid teams help fans on pitch

frightened spectators on the pitch.

A senior police officer said: "On the whole the crowd behaved very well.

"The trouble at the Kop end seems to have happened because many of them could not see—because of a haze.

"This seems to have caused a crush forward which resulted in many people being injured."

Weather expert George Wood, of Swindon Lancashire said last night:

"Perspiration from the huge crowd at the Kop could well have caused the unusual phenomenon.

"It is similar to what happens at a racehorse after a hard run."

Rare

"It has happened at Rugby matches at Cardiff Arms Park where a steam atmosphere has elevated part of the crowd.

"These occasions are rare. But it only happens at big soccer and rugby matches where there are huge crowds."

AXEMAN: YARD SEEK 2 GANGSTERS

By TOM TULLETT and DOUGLAS SLIGHT

LIVERPOOL OUT OF EUROPE

Hunt hits two—but the mountain was too high to climb

By KEN JONES

THE task was too great, the mountain too high to climb.

Liverpool are out of the European Cup.

Roger Hunt beats Ajax goalkeeper Bals to score the first of his two goals for Liverpool.

European Cup (1st round, 2nd leg)

LIVERPOOL	2
Hunt (55 mins, 66 mins)	
AJAX	2
Graaf (50 mins, 71 mins)	
Ajax win on aggregate 7-3	

a record season for Littlewoods winners!

LAST WEEK - BIGGEST EVER TREBLE CHANCE PAYOUT

£751,725

CRICKET

Counties all set for battle

By BRIAN CHAPMAN

IT'S ALL WATFORD —THEN TORQUAY HALT AWAY RUN

John wrecks Fulham in extra time

Fulham 1

Already this season Littlewoods have paid:

1st over	£33,198	10 winners over	£40,000
2nd over	£46,882	16 winners over	£25,000
3rd over	£67,000	17 winners over	£15,000
4th over	£50,000	5 winners over	£10,000
5th over	£45,000	100 winners over	£5,000
1,728 winners over £1,000			

LITTLEWOODS

The match attendance was just short of 54,000 and a packed Kop spilled on to the pitch. On a damp misty December night steam was visibly rising from the famous terrace and many fans were injured in the crush.

95

"Congratulations son, you'll be playing near a great side.
Bill Shankly to Alan Ball after he joined Everton"

Ron Yeats and Tommy Smith move in on Everton's new signing, Alan Ball, Anfield December 1966. The match was a 0-0 draw.

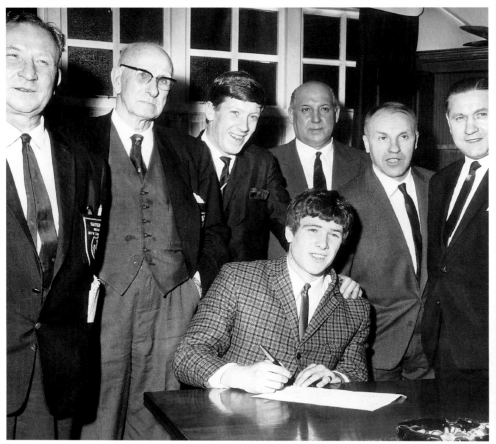

Emlyn Hughes signs for Liverpool from Blackpool for £65,000 in February 1967.

With the 1966-7 season being such a huge disappointment Bill Shankly knew he had to bring new players to complement the team that had served him so well in the past. The defeat against Ajax was the catalyst for change and rebuilding. Inevitably, the great team of the 1960s began to be dismantled. In 1967 Liverpool were busy in the transfer market, buying Emlyn Hughes, Ray Clemence and Tony Hateley.

New signing Tony Hateley was bought from Chelsea for £100,000. He did well at Anfield, scoring once every two games and linked up well with Roger Hunt. His career at Anfield was short-lived though, since he made only 56 appearances. The signing of Alun Evans in 1968 was the writing on the wall: the so-called "wealthy wanderer" was sold to Coventry for £80,000 in September 1968.

Police escort fans away after fighting broke out at Maine Road in August 1967 in the first match of the season between Manchester City and Liverpool. The 1960s saw a rise in crowd disturbances as more and more fans began to travel up and down the country to watch their team.

A fan is given a helping hand off the pitch during the Fulham v Liverpool match at Craven Cottage in 1967.

Liverpool v Ferencvaros. Geoff Strong challenges Pancsics of Ferencvaros in the European Fairs Cup, a forerunner to the UEFA Cup. Liverpool were beaten 1-0 at Anfield and 2-0 on aggregate by the team that formed the nucleus of the Hungarian national side. Snow-covered pitches with the distinctive orange ball were a regular occurrence during midwinter before under-soil heating.

LIVERPOOL
FOOTBALL CLUB / ANFIELD

Honours:
F A Challenge Cup Winners Season 1964/65
Football League Champions Division 1
Season 1900/01   Season 1946/47
Season 1905/06   Season 1963/64
Season 1921/22   Season 1965/66
Season 1922/23

INTER-CITIES FAIRS CUP COMPETITION
THIRD ROUND—SECOND LEG

LIVERPOOL v.
T.C. FERENCVAROS (Hungary)
TUESDAY, 9th JANUARY, 1968
Kick-off 7-30 p.m.

Price 6D

Below: Tony Hateley and Emlyn Hughes relax playing snooker at a Blackpool hotel, watched by local youngsters after news of the Liverpool team staying in the resort spread throughout the town, April 1968.

Above: Liverpool trainer Bob Paisley carries an injured Emlyn Hughes off the pitch, April 1968.

Left: Liverpool players, **left to right:** Alf Arrowsmith, Ian St John and goalscorers Ron Yeats and Roger Hunt enjoying their stay in a Blackpool hotel reading about the match they had just won at Old Trafford, April 1968. Liverpool had just beaten the reigning champions and soon-to-be European champions Manchester United at Old Trafford 2-1.

In 1968 Liverpool bought 18-year-old striking sensation Alun Evans from Wolverhampton Wanderers, the very first £100,000 teenager. He was a blond mop-topped forward with an eye for goal. Quick, strong and full of courage, he was regarded as a star of the future; but a much publicized night club incident that left him facially scarred by a broken bottle and cartilage trouble ended his short career at Anfield. He scored a fantastic hat-trick in the Fairs Cup match against Bayern Munich in March 1971, but that was the highlight of his time at Anfield.

Alun Evans in action for Liverpool.

Alun Evans tries a shot against Manchester United. Liverpool won the match 2-0 with goals from St John and Evans, Anfield October 1968.

Ron Yeats tackles Francis Lee at Anfield, August 1968.

Below left: Liverpool's Emlyn Hughes heads the ball clear from City forward Bobby Owen.

Below right: Liverpool goalkeeper Tommy Lawrence dives to stop a shot by Francis Lee that hit the bar.

Larry Lloyd (left) and Alex Lindsay (right) challenge Ray Kennedy (centre) when he played for Arsenal, November 1970.

With the help of his trusted scouts, ex-player Geoff Twentyman and Tom Saunders, Shankly continued to rebuild his squad, to include new arrivals Alex Lindsay and Larry Lloyd. Larry Lloyd was bought from Bristol Rovers for £60,000 in April 1969. He was a towering dominant centre-half in the Ron Yeats mould. Brave, solid and good in the tackle he was the perfect replacement for Yeats and was an inspiration to Liverpool's defence for more than five years. He was a stalwart of Shankly's "second"

Arsenal keeper Bob Wilson collects the ball, challenged by Larry Lloyd as George

Above: Mick Jones scores against Tommy Lawrence at Elland Road, August 1968. Leeds eventually went on to win the League with Liverpool runners-up.

Right: Liverpool v Burnley League match at Anfield, August 1969. Burnley goalkeeper Peter Mellor saves from a Bobby Graham header.

In the 1968-9 season Liverpool came close to winning the League with this fresh injection of new blood, but a 1-0 defeat at Elland Road and a goalless draw with the eventual champions at Anfield in April 1969 put an end to their title hopes, and they finished six points behind Don Revie's Leeds United. During this period Leeds United emerged as Liverpool's great rivals, and there were many classic battles between the two sides.

Even though he signed as a schoolboy in 1961, Motherwell-born Bobby Graham only became a regular in the 1969-70 season, playing in every League game and scoring 13 goals. He was a Kop favourite but with the arrival of Kevin Keegan and John Toshack he found it difficult to win his place back.

Below: Goalmouth scramble with Tommy Smith, Jack Charlton, Billy Bremner, Tommy Lawrence and Emlyn Hughes as Ian St John looks on. Tommy Lawrence was judged to have brought Bremner down, and a penalty was awarded.

Above: Gary Sprake watches despairingly as a Ron Yeats header goes through his legs and over the line at Elland Road, November 1969.

This wasn't Gary Sprake's worst mistake against Liverpool in this period. At Anfield a couple of seasons earlier, when attempting to throw the ball out Sprake forget to let go and threw the ball into his own net.

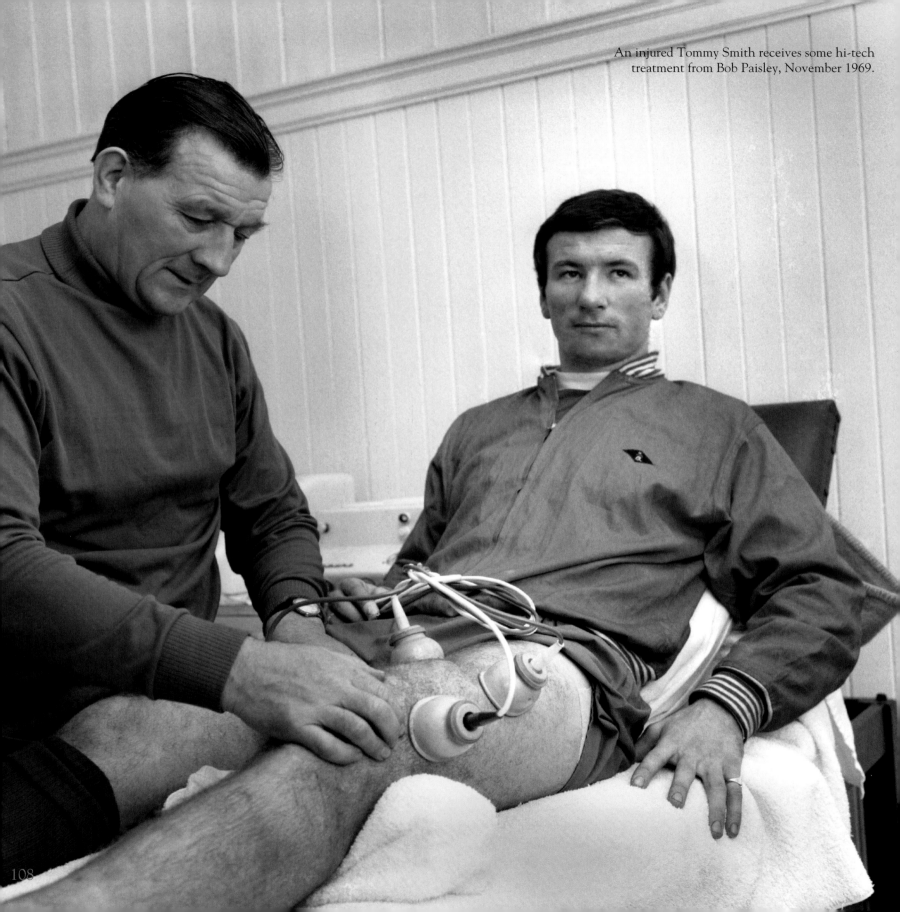

An injured Tommy Smith receives some hi-tech treatment from Bob Paisley, November 1969.

Top: Sandy Brown of Everton scores one of the all-time classic "derby" match own goals with a diving header in December 1969.

Left: Sandy Brown looks forlornly at the ball in the back of the net after his own goal as Brian Labone looks on in disbelief.

Above: Liverpool fans are all smiles in the Park End at Goodison Park. Liverpool won the game 3-0 against the eventual champions.

–LEGENDS–

Roger Hunt

Roger Hunt, dubbed "Sir" Roger Hunt by the Kop, was one of Liverpool Football Club's great all-time goalscorers. For 23 years he held the club goalscoring record of 286 goals before Ian Rush broke it, but he still holds the record for most goals in one season after finding the net 41 times in the promotion campaign of 1961-2. He was alert, a hard worker and always had an eye for goal. He linked up brilliantly with Ian St John in the 1960s and scored many vital goals during his time at Anfield. His average was better than a goal every two games for his club. He was a member of the 1966 World Cup winning team and was so popular that over 56,000 attended his testimonial at Anfield.

Roger Hunt scores against Burnley 1969.

Roger Hunt scores against Southampton, October 1969.

Roger Hunt coming towards the end of his Liverpool career came on as substitute against Southampton at Anfield in October 1969 and is seen here scoring the first of his two goals in two minutes watched by Emlyn Hughes. Liverpool won the game 4-1.

FOOTBALL
–STATS–

Roger Hunt

Name: Roger Hunt

Born: Lancashire 1938

Position: Inside-forward/ striker

Liverpool Playing Career: 1959-1969

Club Appearances: 492

Goals: 286

England Appearances: 34

Goals: 18

Roger Hunt playing in the World Cup final, 1966.

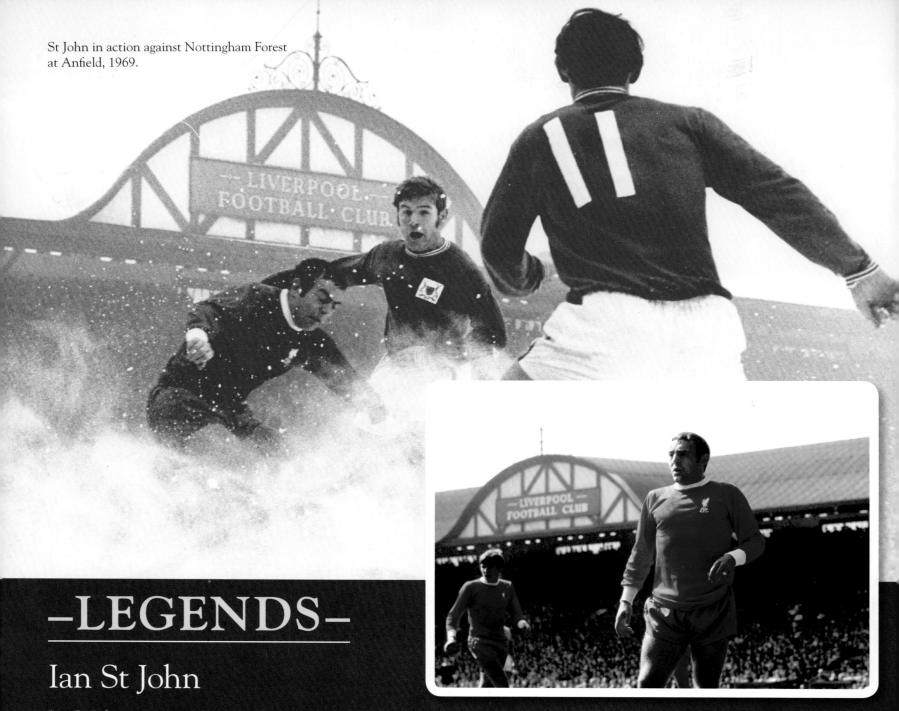

St John in action against Nottingham Forest at Anfield, 1969.

–LEGENDS–

Ian St John

Ian St John was signed from Motherwell in 1961 for a club record fee at the time of £37,500. St John made himself an immediate hero by scoring a hat-trick against Everton in the Liverpool Senior Cup competition at the end of the 1960-1 season. Although small for a centre-forward he was excellent in the air and scored many of his goals with headers, including his famous winner in the 1965 FA Cup final. He struck up an excellent partnership with Roger Hunt and was the perfect foil for Hunt with his darting runs and intelligent passing. Later on in his career he dropped deeper, almost into midfield, but his football brain meant he was still a valuable asset. He left Liverpool for Coventry in 1971 after a brief spell in South Africa. He went on to become a manager and then a TV and radio commentator.

Ian St John playing against Fulham at Craven Cottage, 1967.

Ian St John in action against Inter Milan, 1965.

FOOTBALL
–STATS–

Ian St John

Name: Ian St John

Born: Motherwell 1938

Position: Centre-forward

Liverpool Playing Career: 1961-1971

Club Appearances: 426

Goals: 118

Scotland Appearances: 21

Goals: 9

LIVERPOOL

INSID

IAN ST.

round of the FA Cup by Watford in February 1970, who were in the Second Division at the time, the future looked bleak. This game was the watershed moment when Bill Shankly decided he would have to dismantle the 1960s team and build again. Kop heroes such as Yeats, Hunt and St John were sold, and Shankly produced a masterstroke by buying John Toshack from Cardiff City for £110,000 in November 1970 and Kevin Keegan from Scunthorpe for a mere £35,000 in May 1971. University graduate Brian Hall had been getting groomed in the reserves from 1967 and Steve Heighway, the flying winger, was another graduate recruited from non-League Skelmesdales United in May 1970. The second great Shankly team was finally taking shape.

In the late 1960s as Shankly was slowly rebuilding the team, Liverpool were consistently finishing near the top of the League – so it was slow change rather than a revolution. Some critics thought he was displaying too much loyalty to the core of the team that had won him two championships, the FA Cup for the first time in the club's history and had taken Liverpool from the Second Division to narrowly missing out on the European Cup glory.

Shankly had bought Tony Hateley and Alun Evans, but these signings turned out to be short-term and the players were soon moved on. In this period players like Emlyn Hughes, Larry Lloyd, Ray Clemence and Alex Lindsay had been bought from the lower divisions and were being introduced to the team, but when Liverpool were beaten in the sixth

Above: Steve Heighway signed from non-League Skelmesdale United.

Left: Bill Shankly with John Toshack at Melwood, 1970.

Below: Kevin Keegan bought from Scunthorpe in May 1971 just before the FA Cup final with Arsenal.

The Spion Kop was named after a hill which was the scene of a fierce battle in 1900 during the Boer War. Many Liverpool men served in the Lancashire Fusiliers and had taken part in the battle near Ladysmith, South Africa. Shortly after Liverpool FC had won its second League championship in 1906, chairman John Houlding and club secretary John McKenna decided that a bigger terrace was needed at Anfield. Originally it was a steep cinder bank with wooden steps designed by respected architect Archibald Leitch, but a local journalist and sports editor of the *Liverpool Echo*, Ernest Edwards, suggested that the massive embankment should be called the Spion Kop as it reminded him of the hill where the battle had taken place. Originally the terrace had no roof, but in 1928 a roof was constructed to protect the spectators from the elements and this, with other alterations, meant that 28,000 could now stand on the terrace. The new roof gave the Kop added crowd volume but it would not be until the 1960s that it exploded into song and eventually became the most famous terrace in the world, acclaimed for its vocal support, innovation and humour.

Despite all the changes in the playing staff the new look Liverpool finished the season fifth and beat their local rivals Everton 2-1 in the semi-final of the FA Cup in an exciting comeback after being 1-0 down.

Left: Ian Callaghan takes on Keith Newton in the FA Cup semi-final against Everton at Old Trafford.

Above: Alun Evans scores to equalize for Liverpool.

Right: Brain Hall jumps for joy after he had scored the winner to put Liverpool into the FA Cup final.

Liverpool fans at the FA Cup final, 1971. Liverpool lost the match 2-1 after going ahead through a Steve Heighway goal.

ARSENAL v LIVERPOOL

FOOTBALL ASSOCIATION CHALLENGE
CUP COMPETITION

FINAL

SATURDAY 8th MAY 1971

Kick-off 3 p.m.

Official Programme . . . 10p

Frank McLintock and Tommy Smith toss up at the 1971 Cup final.

Brian Hall takes on George Armstrong in the 1971 FA Cup final against Arsenal.

Kevin Keegan made his Liverpool debut against Nottingham Forest and made an immediate impact, scoring after 12 minutes in front of the Kop. In his first season with Liverpool he was an absolute sensation and his energy and work rate was an inspiration to the rest of the team.

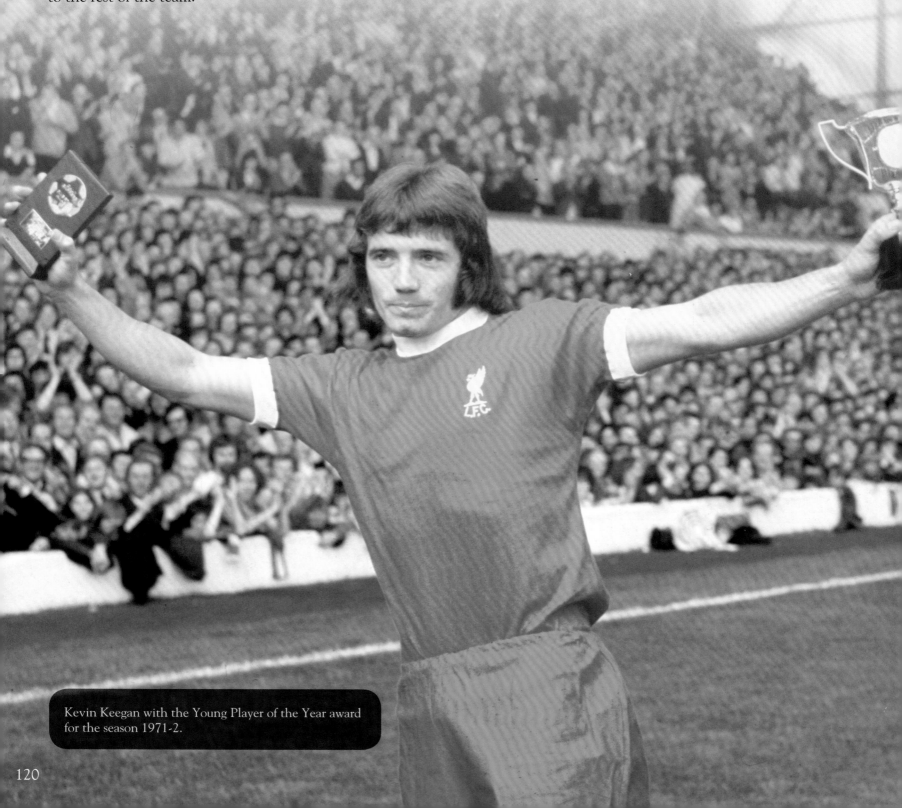

Kevin Keegan with the Young Player of the Year award for the season 1971-2.

Ray Clemence, 1971.

In the 1971-2 season the team was beginning to take shape. A solid defence included goalkeeper Ray Clemence, Chris Lawler, Larry Lloyd, Emlyn Hughes, Tommy Smith and Alex Lindsay. The 1971-2 season was an exciting season but without any silverware to show at the end after Brian Clough's Derby County pipped them to the League. However, there were encouraging signs, mainly due to the blossoming Toshack-Keegan partnership. Liverpool in fact needed to beat Arsenal at Highbury to clinch the championship, but as the Liverpool players and fans celebrated John Toshack's last-minute winner they had failed to notice that the linesman had ruled it offside.

Emlyn Hughes and Tommy Smith with the League Trophy at Anfield, 28 April 1973.

New signing Peter Cormack helped Liverpool win the League in his first season at the club.

In the 1972-3 season Bill Shankly's second great team came of age. With the purchase of the skilful midfield playmaker Peter Cormack from Nottingham Forest for £110,000 in July 1972, the jigsaw was complete. For the first time in seven years Liverpool's team bore a stamp of familiarity: Clemence, Lawler, Lindsay, Smith, Lloyd, Hughes, Keegan, Cormack, Heighway, Toshack and Callaghan. Local youngsters Phil Thompson and Phil Boersma were also challenging for a place in the team as well as the ever dependable Brian Hall. Some of the performances that season were breathtaking, with the emphasis on teamwork, and when Liverpool beat Leeds 2-0 on a scorching hot Easter Monday it was more or less done and dusted. Liverpool were awarded the League trophy at the home match against Leicester in front of 56,000 adoring fans with the gates being locked hours before kick-off. This was the dawning of a new era which would see Liverpool dominate domestically and in Europe for the next two decades.

On this day Bill Shankly was immortalized. He had been adored in the 1960s but this was something special. He had built the foundations of a new dynasty. The mutual adulation between the Kop and Bill Shankly was breathtaking. Shankly's name echoed around the famous terrace long after the final whistle and the lap of honour, to the tune of *Amazing Grace* and those present knew they were witnessing a "communion" unprecedented in the history of the game.

> *The Kop is exclusive, an institution, and if you're a member of the Kop, you feel you're a member of a society, you've got thousands of friends around you and they're united and loyal.*
>
> – Bill Shankly

Above: The Spion Kop, Liverpool v Leicester, 28 April 1973.

Left: Bill Shankly acknowledges the adulation of the Kop after winning the League for the third time.

Above: Tommy Smith leads the team onto the pitch at Anfield in 1972 with his distinctive red boots.

Right: Tommy Smith leaving the dressing room at Anfield clutching the League trophy.

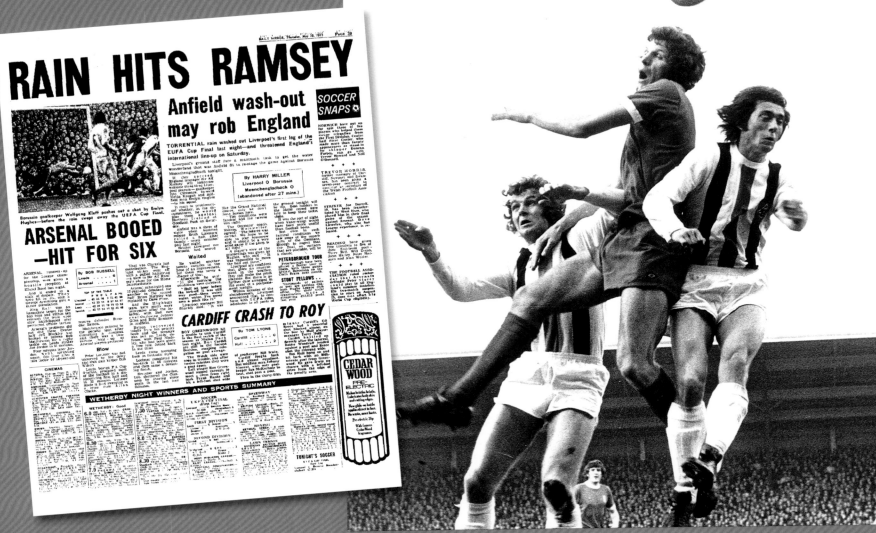

The Liverpool v Borussia Mönchengladbach UEFA Cup first leg was abandoned after torrential rain, but even then the headline writers were more interested in how it affected England's home championship plans.

John Toshack's aerial threat helped Liverpool to a 3-0 home victory in the first leg of the UEFA Cup final.

Liverpool played the first leg of their UEFA Cup final against Borussia Mönchengladbach at Anfield on 9 May 1973. Surprisingly, Bill Shankly left out John Toshack for the home leg, preferring to play Brian Hall instead. However, this match was abandoned after 27 minutes because torrential rain had produced a waterlogged pitch. The game was rearranged to be played the following evening. Shankly and his staff had spotted a weakness in the German defence and the following night Toshack was restored to the line-up. The towering centre-forward was instrumental in destroying Borussia 3-0, setting up two goals for Kevin Keegan. Larry Lloyd made it three with a well-headed goal. Liverpool took a first leg lead to Germany but after the first half-hour the classy Borussia side seemed to run out of steam and despite a 2-0 defeat Liverpool held on to register a famous victory 3-2 on aggregate and Liverpool's first European trophy. Those closest to Bill Shankly revealed that this was one of his proudest moments, mirroring the defeat to Inter Milan in 1965, which had haunted him. This success in Europe undoubtedly laid the foundations for Liverpool's dominance of Europe later in the decade.

Above: Liverpool and Borussia Mönchengladbach 1973: UEFA Cup final second leg match in Munich Borussia Mönchengladbach 2 v Liverpool 0 (Liverpool won 3-2 on aggregate). Liverpool captain Tommy Smith leads out the team, May 1973.

Left: Liverpool bench at UEFA Cup final, 1973.

Winning a European trophy had become an obsession for Bill Shankly after the disappointments in the European Cup in 1965 and the Cup Winners Cup in 1966 and 1971. In those days the UEFA Cup was a very difficult trophy to win as only the champions of each country went into the European Cup and the challenging and emerging teams went into the UEFA Cup.

Above: Liverpool fans at the UEFA Cup final on 23 May 1973. Liverpool fans were well known for travelling in Europe to support their team.

Right: A proud Bill Shankly holding the UEFA Cup, 1973.

Liverpool narrowly missed out on a consecutive League title in the 1973-4 season, finishing five points behind their great rivals Leeds United after the disappointment of being knocked out of the European Cup by a brilliant Red Star Belgrade side 4-2 on aggregate.

Below: Gordon Banks with Bill Shankly, Anfield, August 1973. The Kop always gave opposition goalkeepers a good reception, and when Gordon Banks received an award and Shankly paraded him around the pitch he received a rapturous reception.

Liverpool started the 1973-4 season in confident mood, with Bill Shankly receiving his Manager of the Year award at Anfield.

Bill Shankly, Bob Paisley, Joe Fagan, Ronnie Moran, Reuben Bennett and Tom Saunders.

In 1974 Liverpool reached their third FA Cup final in less than 10 years.

Above: Liverpool and Newcastle United walk on to the Wembley turf before the FA Cup final.

Right: WAGS in 1974 on their way to the Cup final.

Below: No ipods in those days! Liverpool players, **from left to right:** John Toshack, Tommy Smith, Emlyn Hughes and Chris Lawler playing scrabble on their way to Wembley, 1974.

The pre-match build-up was dominated by Malcolm McDonald and his promise to demolish the Liverpool defence; but he hardly touched the ball and when he did Liverpool's defence smothered him.

Top: Malcolm McDonald on one of his rare forays is closely marked by Phil Thompson with Tommy Smith in close pursuit.

Above: Liverpool fans at Wembley for the Cup final in 1974 with the famous "No Way the Lads" flag.

Right: Peter Cormack on the ball is watched by Terry McDermott, then playing for Newcastle. His performance in the Cup final that day convinced Liverpool to try to sign him.

Liverpool celebrate on the pitch after their 3-0 victory over Newcastle, 4 May 1974.

Top: Liverpool fans with a flag "Some Say God, We Say Shankly" in the fountains of Trafalgar Square after winning the Cup at Wembley.

Above: Bill Shankly relaxes on the train home after winning the FA Cup.

High Noon – Shankly Resigns

On Friday 12 July 1974, just over two months after the FA Cup triumph, Bill Shankly stunned Liverpool fans and shocked the footballing world by announcing his retirement. Bewildered fans refused to believe the news, which became Liverpool supporters' "JFK moment". Every Liverpool fan alive at that time can remember where they were when they heard the bombshell that Shanks was calling it a day. Shankly was quoted as saying *"coming to my decision was like walking to the electric chair"*. Various theories and speculations followed his decision to quit football management, but in his autobiography he simply revealed that he stepped down for the sake of his family. In the confusion and chaos of the day it was almost overlooked that Shankly had bought Ray Kennedy from Arsenal for £200,000.

Ray Kennedy signs for Liverpool. **Left to right:** T V Williams (president) Bill Shankly, John Smith (chairman).

Paisley – King Of Europe
1974-1983

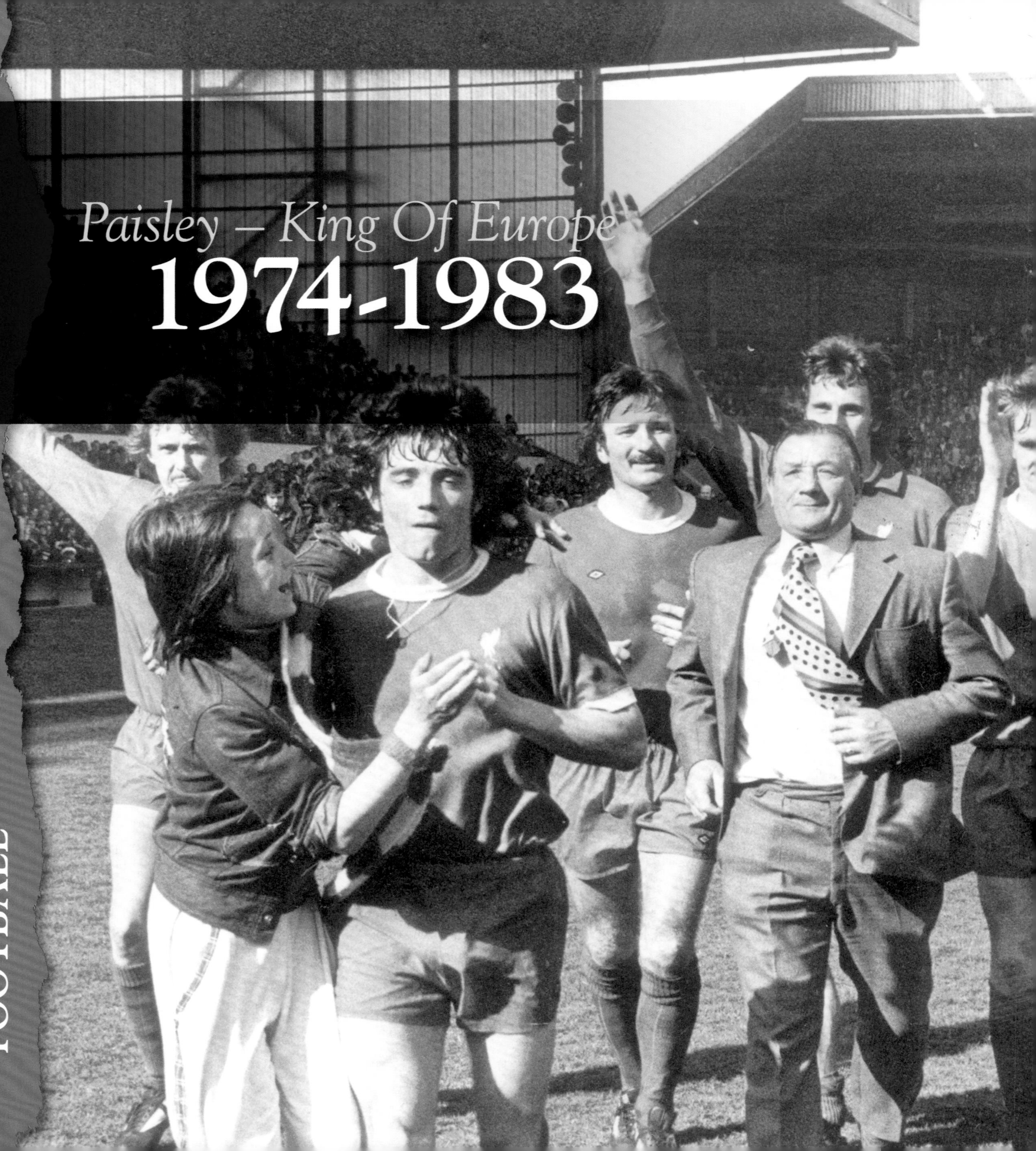

Bob Paisley leads the Liverpool team on a lap of honour in 1974-5. Bob Paisley felt his first season in charge was a failure because he finished second in the League and the team were dumped out of the League Cup at home by Middlesbrough 1-0 and the FA Cup away to Ipswich 2-1. They did however record their biggest win ever in Europe by beating Norwegian amateurs Stromgodset 11-0 at Anfield, but they went out to old rivals Ferencvaros in the next round.

Once the shock of Shankly's resignation had subsided, speculation about his successor was rife. But Bill Shankly had no doubts. He recommended his trusted servant Bob Paisley, who had been a player, physio, trainer and an assistant manager, the man in fact who had attempted to get Shankly to reconsider his momentous decision. The Liverpool Board agreed and Bob Paisley was appointed manager on 26 July 1974, exactly two weeks after Shankly's resignation. Paisley reluctantly accepted the post and described it as the proudest moment of his life; but he also had reservations about succeeding the charismatic legend that was Bill Shankly.

If Bob Paisley regarded his first season as a disappointment his second season in charge was a resounding success. Paisley had quietly been adding to the team Shankly had left behind, and in the autumn of 1974 he brought two newcomers to the club, full-back Phil Neal, who was bought for £60,000 from Northampton Town, and Kirkby-born Terry McDermott, who had impressed for Newcastle in the FA Cup final, was purchased for £170,000. Before the start of the 1975-6 season Paisley signed Joey Jones from Wrexham and brought into the squad two local lads, Jimmy Case and David Fairclough. Ray Kennedy, bought as an out-and-out striker, was switched to a midfield role.

Left: Phil Neal when playing for Northampton Town in July 1969.

Above: Joey Jones was a tough-tackling crowd favourite.

Below Left: Terry McDermott signed from Newcastle in 1974 shortly after playing against Liverpool in the FA Cup final.

Below Right: Ray Kennedy was transformed from a striker into a goalscoring midfielder by Bob Paisley.

Above: Frank McLintock of Queens Park Rangers and Peter Cormack of Liverpool in action at Anfield on 20 December 1975. Though Liverpool won the match 2-0 they were closely challenged for the League in the 1975-6 season by QPR and had to win their final game of the season at Wolverhampton Wanderers to win the League.

Right: In a dramatic finale Liverpool won their final match against Wolves 3-1 with late goals from Keegan, Toshack and Ray Kennedy after being 1-0 down with 15 minutes to go.

Far Right: Emlyn Hughes leads the celebrations in the dressing room after Liverpool clinched the title in the final game of the season.

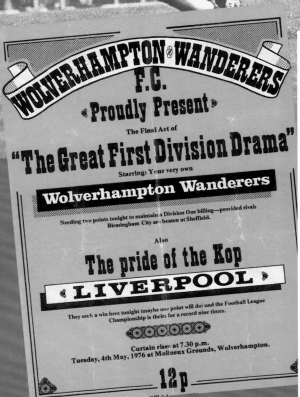

WOLVERHAMPTON·WANDERERS
F.C.
Proudly Present

The Final Act of

"The Great First Division Drama"

Starring: Your very own

Wolverhampton Wanderers

Needing two points tonight to maintain a Division One billing—provided rivals
Birmingham City are beaten at Sheffield.

Also

The pride of the Kop
◆ **LIVERPOOL** ◆

They seek a win here tonight (maybe one point will do) and the Football League
Championship is theirs for a record nine times.

Curtain rises at 7.30 p.m.
Tuesday, 4th May, 1976 at Molineux Grounds, Wolverhampton.

12p

Above: Kevin Keegan scores from the penalty spot in the UEFA Cup final first leg against FC Bruges. After being 2-0 down at half-time Liverpool produced a spirited comeback to win 3-2.

Right: UEFA Cup final first leg at Anfield, April 1976, with David Fairclough of Liverpool being tackled. Liverpool 3 v Club Brugge 2 (Liverpool won 4-3 on aggregate).

Left: John Toshack and Kevin Keegan celebrate after winning the 1976 UEFA Cup.

Fashion Crazy Footballers – 1970s

Top: Steve Heighway with his wife Sue.

Above: Peter Cormack, 1973. Peter Cormack started his own fashion business: here he is wearing some of the clothes he designed himself.

Right: Kevin Keegan in Disneyland, May 1975.

Whereas Tommy Smith sported the classic '70s look at Lancaster Gate at a disciplinary hearing in 1973, Bill Shankly still preferred to adopt the New York "Godfather" look that he so admired.

Graeme Souness, 1975.

-LEGENDS-

John Toshack

Bought from Cardiff City in November 1970 for £110,000, John Toshack was a very skilful centre-forward who was also excellent in the air. He made a slow start to his Liverpool career but with the arrival of Kevin Keegan in May 1971 his fortunes were transformed. His partnership with Keegan was sensational, and over the next six seasons they formed an almost telepathic understanding which demolished domestic and European defences.

Both players scored regularly but also created numerous opportunities for each other. With Toshack's aerial power and Keegan's darting runs they were a lethal combination that helped Liverpool lift many trophies during the 1970s. Toshack left Anfield in 1978 to become player-manager of Swansea City, where he was a tremendous success guiding Swansea from the Fourth to the First Division in successive seasons. His managerial skills have been sought after ever since and he has managed teams across Europe, including the Welsh national team.

Above: John Toshack playing against Arsenal at Highbury, 1970.

Below left: The Keegan-Toshack combination at St James's Park, Newcastle, August 1971.

FOOTBALL -STATS-

John Toshack

Name: John Benjamin Toshack

Born: Cardiff 1949

Position: Centre-forward

Liverpool Playing Career: 1970-1978

Club Appearances: 246

Goals: 96

Wales Appearances: 40

Goals: 12

John Toshack in action against West Ham, August 1972.

145

David Fairclough scores a dramatic late winner against St Etienne to put Liverpool through to the European Cup semi-final in 1977.

Right: Bob Paisley celebrates Liverpool's tenth League title with Emlyn Hughes after the match with West Ham in 1977.

Below: Ray Kennedy, Jimmy Case and Emlyn Hughes parade the First Division trophy. Liverpool retained the title in the 1976-7 season mainly thanks to their brilliant home form at Fortress Anfield.

Kevin Keegan pours a bucket of water over the head of Emlyn Hughes during celebrations.

SORR... ...IAM-AM-EER
NOT EVEN A ...HARP 'EMBLEY- ROME
AS JOEY JONES BITES THE MANCHESTERTARTS THE WORLD ...VERPOOL F...

Liverpool fans at the FA Cup final in 1977, Liverpool v Manchester United.

HERE VE GO

148

David Johnson, a £200,000 signing from Ipswich before the 1976-7 season, in action in the 1977 Cup final.

Jimmy Case celebrates with Kevin Keegan after his goal against Manchester United in the 1977 FA Cup final. Liverpool lost 2-1 after dominating for much of the game, destroying their dreams of a unique League, FA Cup and European Cup treble.

> *We're on our way to Roma on the 25th of May,*
> *All the Kopites will be singing*
> *Vatican bells they will be ringing*
> *Liverpool FC we'll be singing*
> *When we win the European Cup.*

Terry McDermott puts Liverpool ahead in the European Cup final in the Olympic Stadium in Rome. Liverpool bounced back from the disappointment of Wembley with a historic 3-1 win to lift the European Cup for the first time in its history.

Veterans from the 1960s team, Tommy Smith and Ian Callaghan, celebrate. They epitomized the spirit of the club and lifting the European Cup was a fitting climax to their remarkable careers.

Bob Paisley shows some old friends the European Cup and the League Trophy on a visit to his home town of Hetton-le-Hole, County Durham, in 1977.

–LEGENDS–

Kevin Keegan

Kevin Keegan was bought as a possible replacement for Ian Callaghan from Scunthorpe for £35,000 in May 1971. This signing was a shrewd bit of business by Shankly. The energetic Keegan was actually bought as a midfielder but he soon impressed in training and pre-season games playing up front. In one session Shankly asked Ian Ross, a trusted man-to-man maker, to shadow Keegan, but after getting the run-around he asked Ross what he was like to mark. Ross replied, "I couldn't get near him boss, he's too quick", and this convinced Shankly to thrust Keegan into Liverpool's opening game of the 1971-2 season against Nottingham Forest.

Accompanying him up front on his debut was John Toshack. Keegan scored on his debut after 12 minutes, and his understanding with Toshack was instantaneous. Their partnership was devastating: TV commentators would regularly exclaim with much excitement, "Toshack-Keegan one nil"!

FOOTBALL –STATS–

Kevin Keegan

Name: Joseph Kevin Keegan

Born: Armthorpe, Yorkshire 1951

Position: Forward

Liverpool Playing Career: 1971-1977

Club Appearances: 323

Goals: 100

England Appearances: 63

Goals: 21

Peter Bonetti saves from Keegan as David Webb and Alan Hudson look on, September 1973.

Kenny Dalglish signs for Liverpool from Celtic in August 1977 for £440,000. **From left to right:** John Smith, Bob Paisley and Peter Robinson. Paisley needed a replacement for Kevin Keegan who had announced that he was leaving for SV Hamburg shortly after the European Cup final.

Kenny Dalglish was an instant success at Anfield: his class and poise were evident straight away as he scored in his first three games. He went on to become arguably, the best player ever to wear the red shirt. In his first season at Liverpool he scored 20 goals in 42 League games and helped Liverpool lift the European Cup at Wembley for the second year running, scoring a superb goal against Bruges at Wembley.

Dalglish scored the only goal of the match against Bruges with a delightful chip. New signing Graeme Souness helped Liverpool finish the League campaign strongly, but could not prevent Nottingham Forest winning. Forest also beat Liverpool in the League Cup, Brian Clough's side would become great rivals during this period.

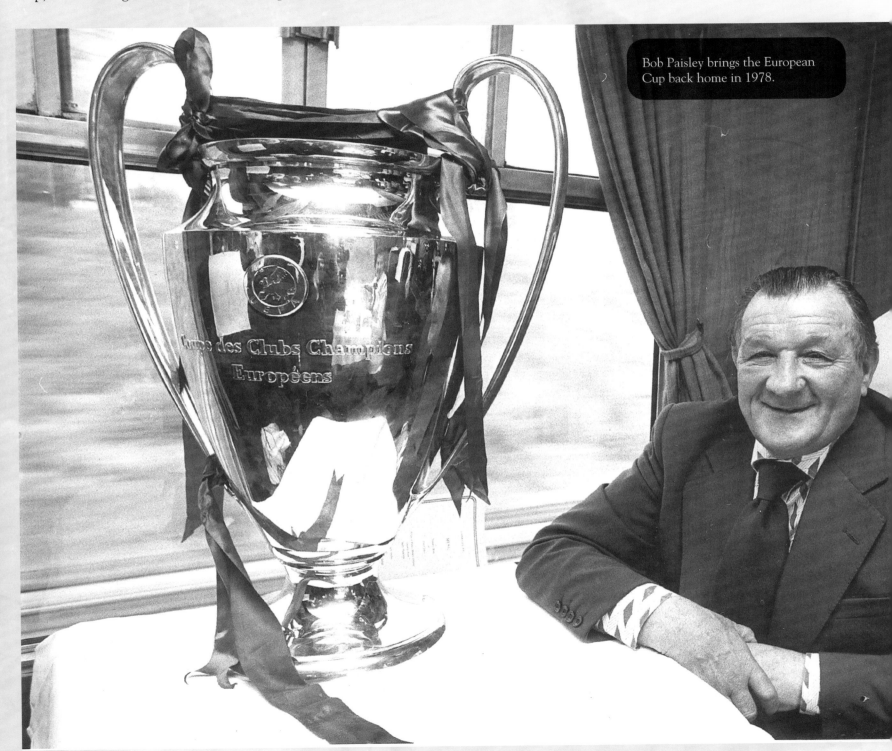

Bob Paisley brings the European Cup back home in 1978.

Jimmy Case tries a spectacular overhead kick against Nottingham Forest in the 1978 League Cup final at Wembley.

Graeme Souness signed from Middlesbrough for £354,000 in 1978. He became the focal point of Liverpool's midfield in the late '70s and early '80s. He was strong, skilful and had a range of passes which made him the engine room of the midfield for six years.

Graeme Souness: Birmingham v Liverpool, September 1980.

Ian "Cally" Callaghan photographed celebrating his 800th appearance for the Reds. He actually went on to play over 850 games for Liverpool before moving to Swansea.

During the summer of 1978 John Toshack left to become player-manager of Swansea City; he also persuaded two Anfield legends, Ian Callaghan and Tommy Smith, to join him.

As the old guard left Anfield, Bob Paisley was busy rebuilding his squad. New additions included Alan Hansen from Partick Thistle for £100,000, Alan Kennedy for £300,000 from Newcastle and Ian Rush from Chester for £300,000. Players who had come through the ranks like Sammy Lee were also beginning to establish themselves.

Right: Alan Hansen (right) when he played for Partick Thistle, 1975.

Sammy Lee was an energetic midfield dynamo. He made his debut in April 1978 and was a squad member until the 1980-1 season when he established himself as a first team regular.

Midfield maestros Graeme Souness and Terry McDermott have plenty to celebrate after winning the League in May 1980 for the twelfth time.

In the 1979-80 season Liverpool's League form was tremendous and they swept all opposition aside. In one match they destroyed a Tottenham team 7-0 at Anfield. They also created the finest defensive record in League history by conceding just 16 goals. Unfortunately, they could not retain the European Cup for the third year in a row, after losing to Nottingham Forest in the first round.

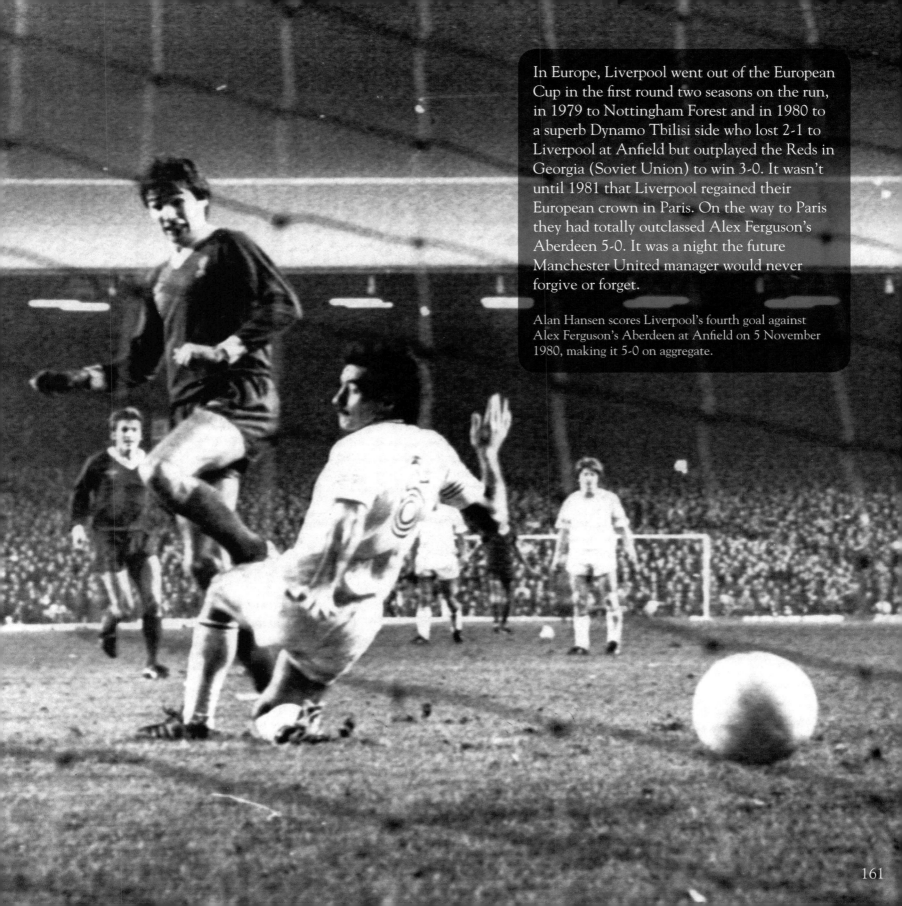

In Europe, Liverpool went out of the European Cup in the first round two seasons on the run, in 1979 to Nottingham Forest and in 1980 to a superb Dynamo Tbilisi side who lost 2-1 to Liverpool at Anfield but outplayed the Reds in Georgia (Soviet Union) to win 3-0. It wasn't until 1981 that Liverpool regained their European crown in Paris. On the way to Paris they had totally outclassed Alex Ferguson's Aberdeen 5-0. It was a night the future Manchester United manager would never forgive or forget.

Alan Hansen scores Liverpool's fourth goal against Alex Ferguson's Aberdeen at Anfield on 5 November 1980, making it 5-0 on aggregate.

The pre-match build-up was dominated by taunts from the manager of Real Madrid. Liverpool won the game 1-0 with a goal from Alan Kennedy.

Sporting Bavarian headgear, Alan Kennedy, Phil Neal, Sammy Lee and Steve Heighway read Phil Neal's book *Attack from the Back* before they met Bayern Munich in the first leg of the European Cup semi-final at Anfield in April 1981. Liverpool drew at home 0-0 then secured their place in the final when they drew 1-1 in the second leg. A late goal by Ray Kennedy stunned the German crowd, with Liverpool going through on the away goal rule to reach their third final in five years.

Alan Kennedy, the scorer of the goal against Real Madrid, kisses the European Cup the day after the match as Phil Thompson, the Liverpool captain, raises a glass.

163

Even though they lifted the European Cup once again, Liverpool did not rest on their laurels and were continually strengthening the squad. They brought in colourful and eccentric goalkeeper Bruce Grobbelaar from Vancouver Whitecaps for £250,000 and Craig Johnston from Middlesbrough for £575,000.

Below: Ian Rush celebrates his goal against Sunderland in the FA Cup fourth round to make it 3-0 to Liverpool.

Bruce Grobbelaar.

In 1981-2 Liverpool started off the League campaign slowly, but when newcomer Ian Rush scored his first hat-trick for the Reds against Notts County in January 1982, they were beginning to climb up the table again. In his first season (1980-1) Ian Rush had looked like an expensive folly, having been signed for £300,000 from Chester. He failed to find the net in seven League games, the replayed Milk Cup final and the first leg of the European Cup semi-final against Bayern Munich. When he was left out of the squad for Paris he called for a meeting with the manager to ask why: Bob Paisley simply replied: "Because you don't score goals so you're not worth your place." Maybe this was the spur the Welshman needed since the following season he was a sensation. He became Liverpool's top scorer and went on to become one of the great goalscorers in the history of Liverpool Football Club.

Bruce Grobbelaar celebrates an Ian Rush goal at Goodison Park. Rush scored four goals against local rivals Everton that day, in a famous 5-0 victory in November 1982.

Alan Hansen and Viv Anderson of Nottingham Forest challenge for the ball as Mark Lawrenson (left) and Phil Thompson (right) look on.

Hansen and Lawrenson formed a partnership that was the bedrock of Liverpool's success in the 1980s.

They marched to their 13th title after a club record of 11 successive victories.

Above: Liverpool win the title in 1982.

Above: Ian Rush takes on the Spurs defence, Milk Cup final, 1982.

Left: Bruce Grobbelaar celebrates Liverpool's Milk Cup victory with a handstand!

Liverpool retained the League Cup, renamed the Milk Cup, having beaten Tottenham at Wembley 3-1 in extra time.

Ray Clemence, the Tottenham goalkeeper, congratulates former team-mate Phil Thompson. Thompson had been superb at the heart of Liverpool's defence for a decade, playing 459 games and leading Liverpool to numerous triumphs.

Peace on the Terraces – What a difference a decade makes!

A tranquil, almost sleepy, scene at the Leeds v Liverpool fixture at Elland Road, 1971.

War on the Terraces!

Just over a decade later it was like a war zone as trouble erupted at Elland Road during the Leeds v Liverpool fixture in February 1982.

Fashion Explodes on the Terraces!

Liverpool fans celebrate at Anfield after beating Everton 3-1, 1981.

The late 1970s and early 1980s was one of the worst periods for football-related hooliganism, and segregated sections and fencing became a common sight in football grounds. The traditional image of the troublesome football fan had well and truly changed. The old "bovver boy" image of the 1970s had been replaced by sportswear and training shoes.

Liverpool fans at the Clock End, Highbury, September 1982.

Liverpool fans had been wearing casual clothing since the 1977-8 season, mostly acquired from their European excursions, but this was the first time they had seen a London team wearing the same type of clothes en masse.

Arsenal fans at the Clock End, Highbury, September 1982.

173

Above: Souness tackles Ossie Ardiles at White Hart Lane, 1982.

Right: Terry McDermott scores from the spot against Arsenal at Anfield in 1981.

Sponsorship started to be common in football during the 1980s. The Football League had first pursued sponsors in the late 1960s, helping to produce new, if rather short-lived, competitions such as the Texaco Cup (1970) and the Watney Cup (1970). The Football League Cup was moved to Wembley in 1967 and became the first major football competition in England to have "named" sponsorship. In 1982 it was renamed the Milk Cup, then the Littlewoods Cup (1986), the Rumbelows Cup (1990), the Coca Cola Cup (1992-3 to 1997-8), the Worthington Cup (1998-9 to 2002-3) and most recently the Carling Cup (2003-4 to present).

Liverpool were in fact the first club to have shirt sponsorship when they signed a deal with Hitachi in 1979. In 1982 Crown paints became the sponsors of Liverpool FC, a relationship that lasted for five seasons, until 1988. Then Candy took over for a few seasons before current sponsors, Carlsberg, started their relationship with the club in 1992-3.

The 1982-3 season was to be Bob Paisley's last in charge. He announced his decision to leave at the start of the season before adding his sixth League title and the Milk Cup to his trophy haul with a win over Manchester United in the final.

Above: Bob Paisley tries out Crown paints products by painting the Paddock at Anfield. Crown paints signed a deal to become Liverpool's sponsor in 1982.

Right: Bob Paisley pours TV presenter Jimmy Hill a cup of milk before the 1983 Milk Cup final.

Bob Paisley relaxes in the boot room after winning the League again.

Kenny Dalglish surrounded by four Manchester United players during the 1983 Milk Cup final at Wembley Stadium. Liverpool won the match 2-1.

Mind, I've been here during the bad times too. One year we came second.
– Bob Paisley

Bob Paisley handed over the reigns to his trusted right-hand man and boot-room "old boy" Joe Fagan. At the press conference Paisley warned the assembled journalists, *"I'll give you a warning. Watch out, the chap who is taking over is a lot hungrier than me"*.

Matt Busby and Bob Paisley parade around Wembley before the 1983 Milk Cup final.

Liverpool players celebrate with Graeme Souness after his goal against Everton in the Milk Cup final replay at Maine Road. It was the only goal of the game after a 0-0 draw at Wembley in the first match.

Top Left: Alan Hansen, Kenny Dalglish and Graeme Souness lift the Milk Cup, Maine Road, 1984.

Above: Graeme Souness lifts the European Cup in Rome, 1984.

Left: Manager of the Year, Joe Fagan relaxes with the European Cup in Rome 1984, the day after the match. In his first year in charge Joe Fagan won a unique treble, the League, the Milk Cup and the European Cup, aided by his trusted lieutenants Ronnie Moran and Roy Evans.

Liverpool players and staff celebrate winning their fourth European Cup after their victory against FC Roma on their home ground. On another memorable European night Liverpool won the match on penalties. It was at the same ground, the Stadio Olimpico, of their first European Cup triumph in 1977.

Trouble starts on the terraces of the Heysel stadium, Brussels, 1985. A chicken-wire fence was all that separated Liverpool and Juventus fans.

The triumphs of the 1983-4 season turned into tragedy at the Heysel stadium on 29 May 1985 when Liverpool faced Juventus in the European Cup final. Weeks before the match Liverpool officials had expressed concerns about the suitability of the stadium, built in the 1930s as an athletics stadium. Peter Robinson the Liverpool chief executive had also called into question the allocation of tickets and the presence of a so-called neutral section in the Liverpool end.

After a carnival atmosphere in Brussels city centre things turned ugly when rival fans began to clash in the stadium in what was meant to be a neutral area but was in fact packed with Juventus fans. The neutral tickets were due to be purchased by locals but had found their way into the hands of Juventus fans. Brussels had a large Italian community and many tickets were snapped up by agencies. It was a scene many had witnessed before and seasoned travellers were not unduly concerned, but soon the trouble escalated and Liverpool fans swarmed over the fence towards the Juventus supporters. Tug-boat flares fired into the retreating masses on the terraces seemed to induce panic and the crowd pressure resulted in a wall collapsing. Some 39 spectators lost their lives in the tragedy, including 32 Italians, four Belgians, two Frenchmen and an Irishman.

Incredibly, the match was played in spite of the fatalities. UEFA wanted the match to proceed as they feared abandoning the game would have led to more trouble. The match was played in a surreal atmosphere with many fans totally unaware of the scale of the disaster. Initially the press blamed Liverpool fans for the carnage but as the facts began to emerge of a woefully inadequate ground and shambolic security arrangements the finger of guilt began to be pointed at the organizers as well. Though some Liverpool fans were indeed culpable some Juventus fans were not without blame either. But innocent

Some years later the Juventus President Giampiero Boniperti recalled that "at noon on the day of the match we made an inspection of the ground and we all tore our hair: it was old, decrepit and it looked like a scrap yard." Many of the organizers were put on trial, including the head of the Belgian FA, the UEFA general secretary and the head of security. However, even though the courts found UEFA responsible they did not prosecute UEFA President Jacques Georges. Instead, they pursued the general secretary who was nearing retirement and was regarded by many as the scapegoat. The trial of those who were supposed to guarantee the organization and safety of the match did not begin until 1988, and, after two appeals and three years of proceedings, only three guilty verdicts were handed out in October 1991 – small suspended sentences. Twenty-five Liverpool fans were extradited to Belgium to face trial for their part in the tragedy. After a five-month trial 14 of these were found guilty of involuntary manslaughter, seven were given three-year prison terms and the remainder received three-year suspended sentences.

In the aftermath, English teams were banned from participating in Europe by UEFA indefinitely and Liverpool for an extra three years after the ban was lifted.

A dark shadow was cast over English football, and Liverpool Football Club in particular on that fateful night. The Heysel tragedy was caused by a combination of factors, poor security arrangements, inadequate segregation, a crumbling stadium and football fans eager and willing to engage and charge at other fans without thought of the potential consequences. The fact is that this match between two of the giants of European football should never have been played in such a dilapidated and dangerous stadium.

Mangled crush barriers and debris litter the dilapidated Heysel stadium terraces the day after the disaster.

Kenny Dalglish celebrates his goal against Chelsea at Stamford Bridge, May 1986. Liverpool won the match 1-0, winning the League.

Liverpool fans celebrate winning the League at Stamford Bridge, May 1986.

Liverpool players rejoice after beating Chelsea 1-0 to win the League at Stamford Bridge, May 1986.

With Liverpool Football Club and football in general reeling from the events at Heysel, Kenny Dalglish was named as player-manager. Liverpool directors had in fact decided on offering Dalglish the job on the eve of the ill-fated Heysel game.

In June 1985 Dalglish became the club's first ever player-manager. After a slow start in the League and a mid-season slump the team put together a tremendous finish to the season, claiming 31 points from their last 11 games. This run put them within touching distance of the title; to lift it they needed to secure a win at Stamford Bridge.

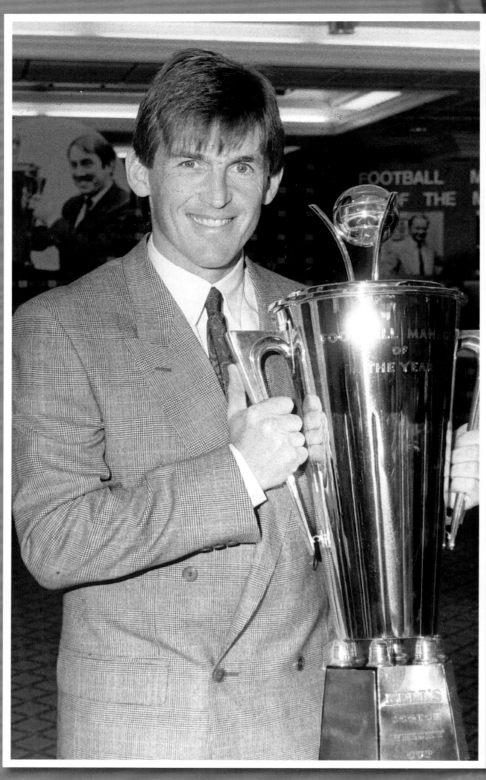

After his first season in charge "King Kenny" was named
Manager of the Year.

Above: Ian Rush celebrates with Jan Molby after his second goal and Liverpool's third to make it 3-1. This goal equalled Dixie Dean's record of 19 goals in derby matches.

Left: Ian Rush celebrates after scoring his first goal against Everton in the 1986 Cup final to make it 1-1.

Liverpool completed the double in the first-ever all Merseyside FA Cup final.

Playmaker and supreme passer of the ball, Jan Molby was superb in midfield on Cup final day. His wide range of passing was never more evident and he ripped open the Everton defence, setting up two of the goals.

Kenny Dalglish looks on pensively as his side crash out 4-1 to Luton in the FA Cup on that plastic pitch once again, having lost there in the League earlier in the season.

In 1988 Peter Beardsley was bought from Newcastle for a British record transfer fee of £1.8 million.

After such a good start to his managerial career Dalglish's team was hounded by inconsistency in the 1986-7 season. They also crashed out of the FA Cup to Luton on their all weather plastic pitch. They did reach the final of the Littlewoods Cup but lost out to Arsenal in the final. It was to be a trophy-less season at Anfield. As this was considered a failure in those days, Dalglish strengthened his squad by buying John Aldridge from Oxford United as a replacement for Ian Rush, who had been transferred to Juventus, John Barnes from Watford and Peter Beardsley from Newcastle.

John Barnes, a £900,000 signing from Watford, was a revelation on the wing for Liverpool.

With these new additions to the squad Liverpool were installed as firm favourites for the 1987-8 season and the football they played that season was among the best that Anfield has ever witnessed.

In the 1987-8 season some of Liverpool's performances were breathtaking and they won three home games on the run in the autumn 4-0. John Aldridge was top scorer with 26 goals, closely followed by John Barnes and Peter Beardsley, both netting 15 each. They finished with 90 points, nine ahead of Manchester United, scoring 87 goals having won 26, drawn 12, and lost just two away from home. The legendary Tom Finney, a great friend and old team-mate of Bill Shankly, was at the League match when Liverpool totally outclassed title challengers Nottingham Forest 5-0 at Anfield in April 1988. Finney said after the game that it was "the finest exhibition I've seen the whole time I've played and watched the game. You couldn't see it bettered anywhere – not even in Brazil. The moves they put together were fantastic". Bill Shankly, who had sadly passed away seven years earlier, would certainly have approved.

Bill Shankly with Tom Finney.

Above: Liverpool celebrate winning the League at Anfield, May 1988.

Right: Wimbledon goalkeeper Dave Beasant is challenged by John Aldridge in the FA Cup final, May 1988.

When Liverpool played Nottingham Forest in the semi-final of the FA Cup at Hillsborough in 1988 the game was a great advert for football, with John Aldridge scoring both goals (one from the penalty spot) in a 2-0 victory. Liverpool fans were packed into the Leppings Lane End at Hillsborough, and all through the match it was noticeable that Liverpool fans were being pulled up into the relative comfort of the stands behind them. Many fans later reported that the tightly packed terrace was causing problems and many had felt uncomfortable. If only the warning signs had been heeded!

Liverpool were only one game away from a second double under Kenny Dalglish, with only Wimbledon standing in their way. Unfashionable Wimbledon were complete underdogs for the final but this physically strong side reliant upon team spirit, aggression and set pieces caused one of the biggest upsets in Cup history by beating Liverpool through a Lawrie Sanchez header. Dave Beasant made a string of superb saves including a second-half penalty from John Aldridge, who was usually deadly from the spot.

The 1988-9 season will be remembered for one event, Hillsborough 15 April 1989. This date is etched into every Liverpool fan's consciousness. On that day, 730 fans were injured, 96 fatally. In 1989, Liverpool FC were paired with Nottingham Forest in the semi-final of the FA Cup just as in the previous year. Once again the FA ignored pleas from Liverpool Football Club (on police advice) to accommodate Liverpool fans in the larger Hillsborough Kop, even though Forest's support was nowhere near as big as Liverpool's. Liverpool, with an allocation of 24,000 tickets had access to 23 turnstiles whereas Forest had an allocation of 29,000 with access to 60 turnstiles. In previous years, most notably 1981, 38 Tottenham Hotspur fans had been injured when a crush had developed on the Leppings Lane terrace. On this occasion the crush had been relieved when police allowed supporters on to the pitch. Hillsborough was not chosen again until 1987, six years after this incident, and both then and in the following year supporters reported being uncomfortable because of overcrowding.

Sheffield Wednesday had made alterations after the 1981 crush and lateral fences were erected to create five pens, but the overall capacity of 10,100 was not reduced. On that fateful day in 1989 a crush developed outside the woefully inadequate turnstiles outside the Leppings Lane End. In 1986 the police had noted that the bottleneck at the turnstiles "didn't provide anything like the access required".

The request was made for a gate to be opened to relieve the crush outside, but no action was taken by police or stewards to direct fans away from the already overcrowded central pens. A sloping tunnel led to these pens, and as fans headed to the terracing a fatal crush ensued. The side pens were well below capacity and if the tunnel had been blocked off and fans directed to these pens this avoidable disaster would never have happened. Liverpool supporters have always maintained that the disaster was due to a complete breakdown in crowd management, decision-making, and communication. The Lord Justice Taylor Report, the public inquiry set up to look into the disaster, supported this view.

After 3,776 written statements, over 1,500 letters, 70 hours of video footage and the evidence of 174 witnesses The Taylor Report found that the "main reason for the Disaster was a failure of police control". Liverpool fans had initially been blamed for causing the crush by inaccurate news reports that they had forced open the gates. These reports were based on false information provided by the Chief Superintendent David Duckinfield who was in command of operations on the day. It was actually his orders to open Gate C which led to the fatal crush and Liverpool fans were exonerated by the Lord Justice Taylor Report when the facts were revealed. Lord Justice Taylor did not find a shred of evidence that police and the rescue services had been prevented from carrying out their duties as reported in the press. These allegations were later called "disgraceful lies" by Lord Justice Stuart Smith in a scrutiny ordered by Home Secretary Jack Straw in 1997 to look into new evidence.

In fact, Lord Justice Taylor called their response to the unfolding disaster "magnificent", praising them for initiating a rescue operation. He blamed the FA for its "ill considered choice of venue", Sheffield City Council for its failure to amend or revise the ground's safety certificate, Sheffield Wednesday FC for its "unsatisfactory and ill-suited" terracing and the confusing and inadequate signposting both inside and outside the ground. However, he reserved his most damning criticism for the person responsible for police operations that day, Chief Superintendent David Duckinfield. Taylor concluded that the man in control of operations who had ordered the gate to be opened without blocking off access to the already overcrowded central pens was a "blunder of the first magnitude".

Liverpool fans help fellow fans out of the crush in the Leppings Lane terrace, Hillsborough 1989.

Left: Kenny Dalglish watching the horror unfold at Hillsborough, 15 April 1989.

Below: Liverpool fans at Hillsborough, 1989.

Liverpool fans initiate and take control of the rescue operation, taking victims across the pitch on advertising hoardings.

Top Left: Scarves and flags, especially from local rivals Everton, adorn a goal at Anfield.

Top Right: A sea of flowers spread across the pitch at Anfield a few days after the disaster. Within a few days the whole Kop and pitch were covered with flags, scarves and flowers from clubs all over the world.

Left: Floral tributes and scarves were also left outside the Leppings Lane End at Hillsborough.

Right: Kenny Dalglish and children Paul and Kelly, with John Smith the Liverpool chairman at the Hillsborough Memorial Service at Liverpool's Anglican Cathedral.

The whole community in Liverpool was in deep shock at the loss of life, and memorials were held throughout the city. As the city as a whole came to terms with its grief and before the deceased had even been buried *The Sun* newspaper printed a front page ludicrously entitled "The Truth". It claimed that Liverpool fans had hampered the rescue operation, assaulted police and St John's ambulance workers, and had stolen from the dead. Both the Taylor Report and the Stuart Smith scrutiny dismissed these allegations and not one police or witness statement ever made reference to any such incidents. The truth was quite the opposite, that Liverpool fans had initiated and coordinated the rescue operation. Since 1989 there has been a sustained boycott of *The Sun* newspaper by footballing fans, which continues to the present day. The newspaper lost 80 per cent of its sales on Merseyside and its circulation has never recovered despite numerous promotion attempts. When Kenny Dalglish was asked how the newspaper could make amends he told them to print a similar headline saying "We Lied", but this was never forthcoming.

Liverpool fans with a "Merseyside Thanks Glasgow" flag at Celtic Park, May 1989. A friendly match was arranged following the Hillsborough disaster in which the friendship and sympathy from the Celtic fans and the people of Glasgow in general were magnificent. Thousands of Liverpool fans made the journey to Glasgow and were overwhelmed by the Glaswegians' empathy. All proceeds from the match went to the victims' families.

Bruce Grobbelaar and Stevie Nichol with their wives at the Hillsborough Memorial Service.

Liverpool and Celtic fans at the Hillsborough Memorial Match, 1989.

Liverpool played Celtic and both sets of fans were allowed to mix together without segregation.

John Barnes is seen here in action against Celtic playing in the Hillsborough Memorial Match, May 1989. This was the first match Liverpool played after the disaster.

John Aldridge scores Liverpool's first against Everton in the 1989 FA Cup final after just four minutes.

Liverpool reluctantly played the rearranged semi-final at Old Trafford on 7 May, three weeks after the Hillsborough disaster. Many fans thought that the FA Cup should have been shelved that year and there was much debate over the best way to commemorate the fans who had lost their lives. The Football Association had been trying to persuade Liverpool to continue in the competition, and after consulting with the families of the bereaved Liverpool decided to take part and, if they won, to dedicate the trophy to the memory of those who had died. Liverpool did win the rearranged semi-final 3-1 and so faced local rivals Everton at Wembley once again.

Ian Rush scoring Liverpool's second in the FA Cup final against Everton, 1989.

Liverpool beat Everton 3-2 after extra time in an emotional final. It was a beautiful day, not unlike that fateful day at Hillsborough five weeks before. The game lived up to expectations and it was a thoroughly entertaining affair, but it was also tinged with sadness as fans' thoughts turned to the tragic events at Hillsborough.

Before the title decider against Arsenal two of their players, Kevin Richardson (left) and Perry Groves lay flowers in the Kop goalmouth at Anfield, May 1989.

Michael Thomas scores Arsenal's second goal at Anfield and wins the title for the London club.

Steve McMahon and John Barnes are inconsolable after Michael Thomas scored a dramatic late goal.

In one of the most sensational finales football has ever witnessed, Arsenal snatched the title from under the noses of Liverpool to deny the "Reds" the double. Arsenal were three points behind Liverpool and had to win by two clear goals to get their hands on the trophy as Liverpool had a superior goal difference. Deep into injury time, with Liverpool 1-0 down and the Kop baying for the final whistle, Arsenal launched one last attack and the ball broke free from a ricochet and Michael Thomas seized his chance and slotted the ball past Grobbelaar to stun the Anfield faithful. Arsenal had won the title with the last kick of the game; however, despite their huge disappointment Liverpool fans gave the Arsenal team a generous and sporting ovation.

John Barnes tries an overhead kick against Norwich, 1990.

Liverpool champions, April 1990.

Liverpool returned to winning ways by lifting the championship the next year. Ian Rush returned from Juventus in Italy and John Aldridge was transferred to Real Sociedad a month into the season. After a hesitant start to the season they demolished Crystal Palace at Anfield 9-0 with goals from Nicol, McMahon, Rush, Gillespie, Beardsley, Aldridge, Barnes and new signing, Swedish centre-back Glenn Hysen, who had been signed from Fiorentina. The star of the 1989-90 season though was John Barnes who won the Footballer of the Year award. He was quite simply unplayable and terrorized defences up and down the country.

201

FA Cup fifth round replay at Goodison Park, 20 February 1991, Everton 4 Liverpool 4 after extra time. **Left to right:** Jan Molby, Gary Ablett, Graeme Sharp, Glenn Hysen, Pat Nevin, David Burrows, Barry Venison and Dave Watson. This was the last match in charge for Liverpool manager Kenny Dalglish, who handed in his resignation the following day.

In 1991 Graeme Souness was appointed manager of Liverpool and made Liverpool legend Ronnie Moran his assistant manager. He won the FA Cup in 1992 but angered fans because he sold an exclusive to *The Sun* newspaper.

Tormentor turned hero! Michael Thomas, who scored the opening goal of the 1992 FA Cup final which helped Liverpool beat Sunderland 2-0. We see him here on the homecoming team bus holding the Cup aloft with the other goalscorer, Ian Rush. Thomas had been bought from Arsenal by Liverpool manager Graeme Souness in 1991 for £2million.

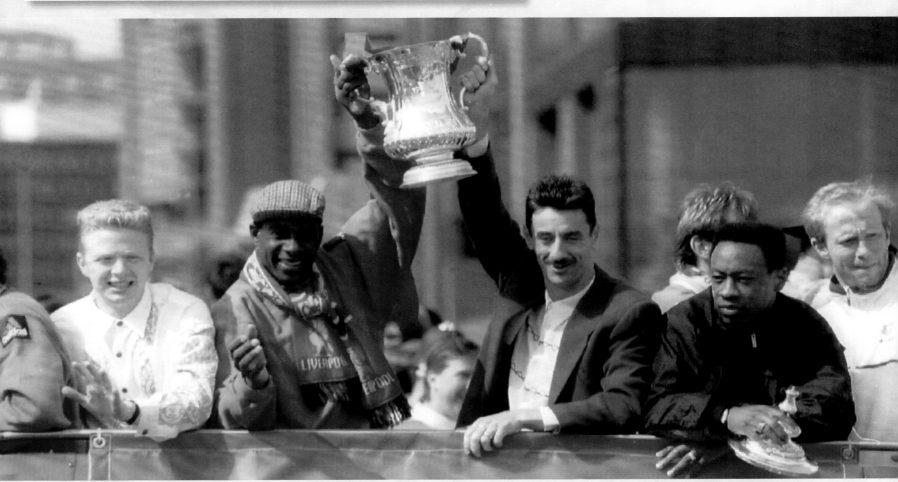

—LEGENDS—

Kenny Dalglish

Kenny Dalglish is regarded by most Liverpudlians as the greatest player ever to pull on a red shirt. King Kenny, the "lad with the golden hair", was already a legend for Glasgow Celtic when he signed for Liverpool in August 1977 for £440,000. The price tag was a record between two British clubs at the time, but Bob Paisley's replacement for Kevin Keegan was worth every penny. With his skill and vision Dalglish was an instant hit with the Anfield faithful. His ability to shield the ball with his back to goal was one of his many attributes. He possessed a superb football brain which would bring out the best in his team-mates and he scored some classic goals. His first touch was instantaneous and even though he was not the quickest when it came to pace he always seemed to be two steps ahead of most opponents on the pitch. His selfless defence, splitting passes for team-mates, became his calling card and he formed fantastic partnerships initially with David Johnson in the late 1970s and then Ian Rush in the 1980s. After the Heysel disaster in 1985 he was made player-manager, a surprising but popular appointment, and won the League and FA Cup double in his first year in charge. As his playing appearances diminished in the late 1980s he was responsible for managing the 1988 team, which many regard as Liverpool's finest ever. Even without his managerial successes he would still be regarded as one of Liverpool's greatest ever legends.

Kenny Dalglish, 1981.

Kenny Dalglish in action against Man United, Charity Shield 1977.

FOOTBALL
–STATS–

Kenny Dalglish

Name: Kenneth Mathieson Dalglish

Born: Glasgow 1951

Position: Centre-forward

Liverpool Playing Career: 1977-1991

Club Appearances: 515

Goals: 172

Scotland Appearances: 102

Goals: 30

-LEGENDS-

Ian Rush

Ian Rush is quite simply the greatest goalscorer in the history of Liverpool Football Club. After being recommended by trusted club scout Geoff Twentyman as a number of clubs pursued him, he was bought in 1980 by Bob Paisley for £300,000 from Chester City. It was a record fee for a British teenager at the time. Rush made a slow start, failing to score in his first seven games, and so rumours began to circulate that Liverpool would cut their losses and sell him. But following a heart-to-heart meeting with Bob Paisley, who told him he should concentrate on hitting the back of the net rather than playing possession football and laying the ball off, his fortunes soon changed and he became a prolific goalscorer, forming a breathtaking partnership with Kenny Dalglish.

His tally against local rivals Everton (25 goals) is a club record and he scored four against them in one match at Goodison in 1982. In the 1983-4 season he scored a remarkable 47 first team goals in all competitions. He was transferred to Italian giants Juventus in 1987 but spent only a year with them, returning to Anfield to continue scoring goals and collecting medals. He left Anfield in 1996 and played out his career for Leeds, Newcastle and Wrexham.

Ian Rush and John Aldridge celebrate, 1989.

Ian Rush beats Frank Lampard (snr) and Phil Parkes to score Liverpool's third goal, Anfield, March 1983.

Liverpool v Leeds, 1981. Rush scores his second goal.

FOOTBALL
–STATS–

Ian Rush

Name: Ian James Rush

Born: St Asaph, Wales 1961

Position: Centre-forward

Liverpool Playing Career: 1980-87 & 1988-1995

Club Appearances: 660

Goals: 346

Wales Appearances: 73

Goals: 28

In 1992 it was Liverpool FC's centenary. They celebrated the 100th anniversary by dressing in period kits.
Back row, left to right: Jan Molby, John Barnes, Bruce Grobbelaar, Steve Nicol and Mark Wright.
Front row left to right: David Burrows, Ray Houghton, Ian Rush, Dean Saunders, Rob Jones and Ronnie Whelan.

Liverpool Football Club had been in existence 100 years and from modest beginnings had grown into one of the
most famous sporting institutions in the world.

MirrorPix Photographic Research – David Scripps, John Mead, Vito Inglese, Alex Waters, and Manjit Sandhu

Liverpool Post and Echo
Thanks for supplying images on pages 6, 7, 8, 9, 10, 11, 12, 16, 24, 25

Thanks – Paul Moreton of Bell Lomax Moreton and to Richard Havers.

Adrian Killen/The Liverpool FC Museum Collection and Stephen Done at The Liverpool FC Museum.

My wife Geraldine, and children Tom and Ella.
My dad for some of the memorabilia and for bringing me up as a Liverpudlian.